Tole-Painte
Outdoor
Projects

Tole-Painted Outdoor Projects:

Decorative Designs for Gardens, Patios, Decks & More

Areta Bingham

Sterling Publishing Co., Inc. New York

A Sterling / Chapelle Book

Chapelle, Ltd.:
- Owner: Jo Packham
- Editor: Laura Best
- Designer: Amber Hansen
- Photography: Kevin Dilley for Hazen Photography
- Staff: Marie Barber, Ann Bear, Kass Burchett, Rebecca Christensen, Marilyn Goff, Holly Hollingsworth, Susan Jorgensen, Barbara Milburn, Linda Orton, Karmen Quinney, Leslie Ridenour, Cindy Stoeckl, Gina Swapp

If you have any questions or comments, please contact:
Chapelle, Ltd., Inc., P.O. Box 9252, Ogden, UT 84409
(801) 621-2777 • (801) 621-2788 Fax
e-mail: chapelle@chapelleltd.com
website: chapelleltd.com

Library of Congress Cataloging-in-Publication Data

Bingham, Areta.
    Tole-painted outdoor projects : decorative designs for gardens, patios, decks & more / Areta Bingham.
        p. cm.
    "A Sterling / Chapelle Book"
    ISBN 0-8069-4486-2
    1. Tole painting 2. Garden structures. I. Title.

TT385 .B54 2000
745.7'23--dc21   99-087166

10 9 8 7 6 5 4 3 2 1

First paperback edition published 2001 by
Sterling Publishing Company, Inc.
387 Park Avenue South, New York, NY 10016
©2000 by Chapelle Ltd.
Distributed in Canada by Sterling Publishing
c/o Canadian Manda Group, One Atlantic Avenue, Suite 105
Toronto, Ontario, Canada M6K 3E7
Distributed in Great Britain and Europe by Cassell PLC
Wellington House, 125 Strand, London WCR2 0BB, England
Distributed in Australia by Capricorn Link (Australia) Pty. Ltd.
P.O. Box 704, Windsor, NSW 2756 Australia
Printed and Bound in China
All Rights Reserved

Sterling ISBN 0-8069-4486-2 Trade
                0-8069-4735-7 Paper

Introduction

This book brings together some of Areta Bingham's most inspired outdoor projects. The step-by-step instructions, color worksheets, and detailed patterns aid in creating beautiful tole-painted projects. Decorate tables, vases, candleholders, and stepping stones, on a variety of surfaces such as galvanized tin, wood, and rock.

The real beauty of these projects is in the simplicity of the painting techniques and the resplendent use of color.

One of the wonderful things about this book is the myriad of different flowers, leaves, and outdoor elements to choose from—whether you follow Areta's instructions exactly or choose to paint other surfaces with a mixture of her techniques, the designs are breathtaking and the applications are endless.

Tole Painted Outdoor Projects is written for the reader who already has a general knowledge of tole-painting. The projects in this book go beyond the basics of tole-painting to decorate the garden, and delight the outdoors.

Remember, no two artists work the same way and you should not expect to reproduce carbon copies of the projects in this book. Put your own personality, skill, and imagination into each project and create your own beautiful and unique treasures.

Contents

paints
brushes
sponge
palette
stylus

Supplies

Many of the supplies necessary for the projects in this book may already be in your studio. Feel free to substitute paint colors and brands, brush sizes, and other materials.

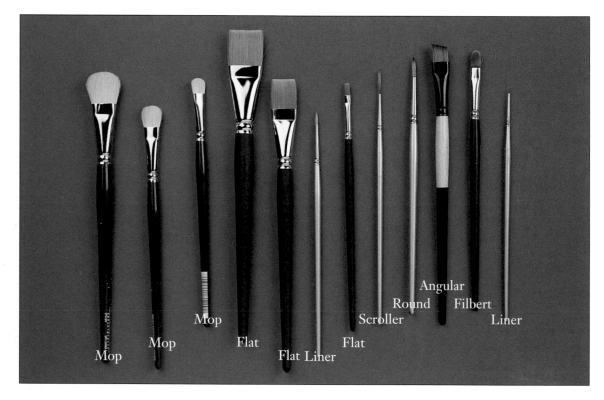

Mop Mop Mop Flat Flat Liner Flat Scroller Round Angular Filbert Liner

Brushes

Use whatever brush is most comfortable for you. Incorporate the largest brush possible for the area to be painted. Listed below are the brushes used on projects in this book.

Angular shaders: ½", ⅜"—used for floating

Filberts: #4, 6, 8, 10—used for stroking flower petals or tinting

Flat shaders: #4, 6, 8, 10, 12—used for base-coating, side-loading, and floating

Liner: #1—used for small detailing

Mop brush—used for blending and softening

Scruffy flat brush—used for stippling and dry-brushing

Retarder brush: ½" flat—used for applying retarder

Round brushes: #3, #5—used for stroke work

Scroller or script: #5/0, 10/0—used for fine lines and detailing

Varnish brush: 1" flat—used to apply varnish

Wash brushes: ½", ¾", 1"—used for base-coating and floating large items

Paints

Acrylic paints are high-quality, bottled acrylic colors. Their rich, creamy formulation and long open time make them perfect for decorative painting. Cleanup is easy with soap and water.

Waterproof, fade-proof exterior acrylics are made especially for projects which will be in the elements. However, projects which may receive a lot of direct sunlight or water may need to have varnish reapplied seasonally.

Gouache is a French term for opaque watercolors. The gouache used on projects in this book are acrylic, water-resistant, and will not chip or crack when cured. Like other acrylic paints and mediums, they have the added benefit of drying through each other. There is no need for initial layers to cure completely before additional painting commences, such as when using oil paints. As with any water-based acrylic product, these paints and mediums should not be used over any oil-based product.

Products from a number of respected paint companies were used when making the projects in this book. In each project supply list, the letter following the paint color represents which company makes the particular color used.

A=Americana
D=Delta
L=Aleene
P=Plaid

The Paint Conversion Chart on pages 139–141 lists the paints used throughout the book and converts them into other paint companies' color equivalents.

Miscellaneous Supplies

Art eraser—to remove pattern lines

Black permanent marker—to trace patterns

Blow dryer—to speed drying

Low-tack masking tape—to secure patterns

Palette knife—to mix paints

Paper towels—to wipe brushes and clean up

Retarder—to slow down drying time

Ruler—to measure placement

Sandpaper or sanding ovals (various grits)—to remove rough spots from painting surfaces

Satin exterior varnish—to protect projects

Sea sponge—to sponge paint

Sponge brushes—to apply paint

Sponge roller—to apply paint or varnish

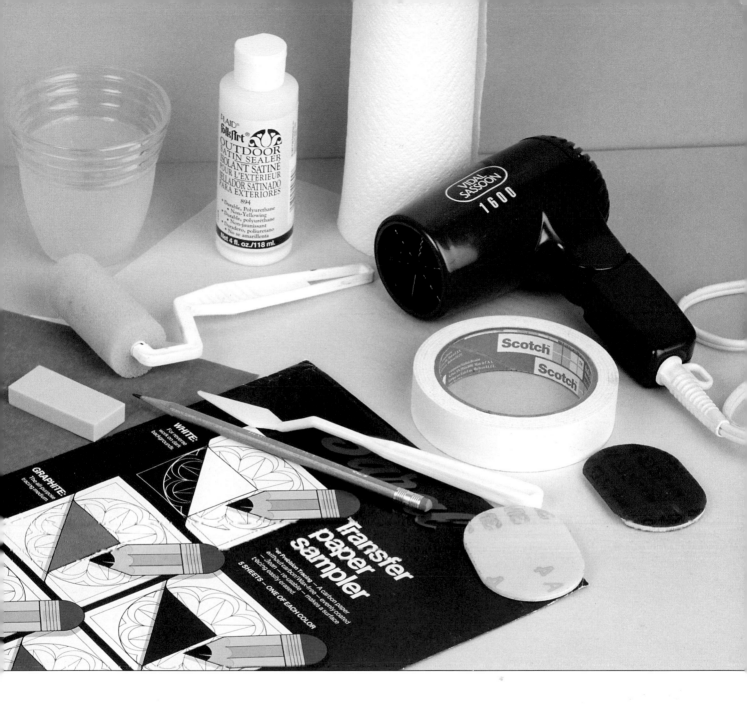

Stiff stencil brush or toothbrush—to fly speck

Stylus—to transfer patterns and apply dots of paint

Tack cloth—to remove sanding dust from wood

Tracing paper—to trace patterns from book

Transfer paper—to transfer patterns onto surface

Water container—to rinse brushes

Waxy palette—to arrange and mix paints

Wood filler—to fill holes and gaps in wood

Wood sealer—to prepare surface before painting

(See individual project instructions for additional supplies needed.)

11

Basic Painting Techniques

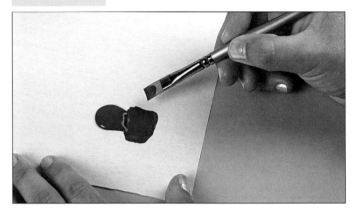

Load

Stroke brush back and forth in paint until brush is full.

Side-load

Dip brush into water, then touch to a paper towel until bristles lose their shine. Pull one side edge of brush through puddle of paint. Stroke brush in same place on palette until there is full-strength paint on one edge and clear water on the other.

Double-load

Dip one side edge of lightly dampened brush into paint, covering about half the width of brush. Dip other side of the brush into a different color. Stroke loaded brush on palette to soften color from side to side. Blend both sides of brush.

Dry-brush

Use dry, worn brushes. Pick up a small amount of paint, then brush over paper towel to remove excess and work paint into bristles. Scrub over project where highlights are needed.

Base-coat

1. Cover an entire area with one initial coat. The paint must be smooth, without ridges or brush strokes. Start in center of project and paint out to edges to prevent ridges on edges. Project may require additional coats for opaque coverage.

2. Light coats of paint will prevent ridges in the overall area. A heavier coat of paint does not cover faster, it just looks messier. Leave base coat as background or shade and highlight on top of base coat.

Slip-slap

Apply and blend two or more colors together by using a criss-cross brush motion. It works best to use the largest flat brush possible for the area to be painted. Avoid overblending the colors.

Wash

Mix paint with water until well blended. The more water used, the more transparent; the less water used the more opaque. Apply a wash of color, then let it dry. If project needs more color, apply another wash.

First Shade

Shading adds depth to painting. Side-load and blend brush on palette. The first shading color will establish shadow areas and create shape and contour. Outside edges can also be defined. The first shade color can also be repeated to create the depth desired.

Third Shade

Sometimes a third value will be needed. This will be done like the second value, but will cover even a smaller area and will only be done where there was a second shading. It will be used to define the deepest, darkest recesses.

Wet on Wet

While the base color is still wet, pick up a second color and blend into the first color. It is best to retard the dry painting surface, then apply several colors as needed. This makes it easier to soften and blend since the entire surface is wet.

Second Shade

Use a darker value, then look for the areas that have already been shaded and deepen them. Keep second shading smaller than previous shading or work will be dark and muddy looking.

Shade or Highlight with Mop

Coat the surface with a retarder. Side-load the shade color and float on shading. Mop the shadow out softly. Repeat until the desired results are achieved. Be certain to let area dry each time before proceeding. Use the same method when highlighting. Avoid using a wet brush. Scrub mop brush over a wet paper towel to remove most of previous color.

Highlight

Much like shading, load brush with water then blot on paper towel. Side-load brush with highlight color, and apply to design. Two or three layers are usually required.

Dot

Make tiny dots by dipping the smaller end of a stylus or bristle tips of a scroller into paint, then touching the project. For bigger dots, use the end of any paintbrush handle. To make dots uniform reload for every dot. For various sized dots, make as many dots as desired before reloading paint.

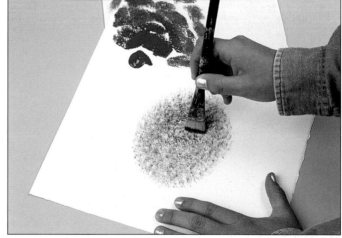

Stipple

Pick up paint in the tips of the bristles of a worn, flat paintbrush. Tap bristles up and down on palette to remove excess and work paint into bristles, then tap on project.

15

Tint

Tinting adds touches of color for interest and depth. The easiest way to tint an item is to use retarder. Use a brush for retarder only, keep it free from water. Dip a dry brush into a small container of retarder; touch brush to a paper towel. Apply retarder to desired area. The area should look satiny, not wet and shiny. It is important not to use too much retarder or paint will run.

Load a small amount of paint on a filbert and apply paint to desired area. To soften color, lightly brush with a mop brush to blend out. If not satisfied, paint will wipe right off so you may start again. Let retarder and paint dry. A hair dryer can be used to speed up the process. Let surface cool down before proceeding.

Apply retarder and repeat as often as necessary to get the desired effect. This method can also be used to shade or highlight, using a flat brush loaded with retarder instead of water, then side-load in desired color. Use a mop brush to soften.

Scrolls or Fine Linework

Using a script brush, scroller, or liner, fully load bristles in inky paint. Pull brush away from puddle of paint and roll brush slightly to make a nice point. There can be a lot of paint in the brush but not on the tip. If paint is the right consistency it will flow like ink.

A liner will not pull strokes as long as a scroller or script brush because the hairs are not long enough to hold much paint. It is best to pull lines in flowers from the center out to the petals. Vein leaves from stem toward tip. Scrolls and tendrils are easier to do if you pull the brush toward you. Balance hand on little finger and forearm not just fingers.

Note: Do not trace lines for scrolls or tendrils. It is much easier to freehand these items than to follow a pattern line.

dust

clean

transfer

trace

sand

Surface Preparation

Galvanized Metal & Tin

Galvanized metal has an oily film that must be removed before painting. Using a moistened cloth, wash metal surface with a mixture of equal parts of vinegar and water, do not immerse piece in water. Let dry. Using fine (180–220 grit) sandpaper, sand lightly to roughen surface. Wipe with a tack cloth.

Spray tin with several light coats of metal primer, following manufacturer's instructions. Let dry 24 hours before proceeding.

Plastic

Using extrafine (220–400 grit) sandpaper, sand rough areas on pots. Wipe away dust and make certain all areas are clean and dry. To prevent plastic from scoring and marring, use a sandpaper made specifically for plastic.

Spray with a bonding agent or apply a coat of gesso before proceeding.

Rocks & Cement

Using a cloth and cool water, wash rocks or cement surfaces to remove dirt and residue. Let dry.

Terra-cotta

Be certain all areas are clean and dry. If painting directly inside pot, it will first need to be sealed on the inside and outside to waterproof. Brush acrylic sealer on both sides and let dry before base-coating.

Wood

Fill nail holes and dents with wood filler. Let dry. Using medium (80–100 grit) sandpaper, sand entire wood piece. Using extrafine (220–240 grit) sandpaper, sand area to be painted. Wipe with tack cloth to remove dust. Seal wood with one coat of wood sealer, following manufacturer's instructions. Let sealer dry.

Using very fine (320–400 grit) sandpaper, sand and tack again before painting. The painting will only be as nice as the time taken to prepare the surface. When base-coating, use as many coats as necessary to cover. Sand final base coat with a brown paper bag.

Pattern Application

Many of the patterns for the projects in this book have been reduced in order to give the maximum number of patterns possible. Enlarge pattern on photocopier according to percentages given. Adjust the size to accommodate the painting surface.

Using a black permanent marker, trace adjusted pattern onto tracing paper. Position tracing paper on painting surface and tape one edge with masking tape. Slide transfer paper underneath tracing paper and lightly trace pattern lines with a stylus. After base-coating project, it may be necessary to retrace detail.

Note: Do not press stylus too hard or it will dent wood.

Painting Tips

Working with Acrylics
• Squeeze paint onto palette, making a puddle of paint about the size of a nickel.

• Pull color with brush from edge of puddle. Avoid dipping brush in center of puddle, putting too much paint on edges.

• Let each coat dry before applying another coat.

Painting Mediums

Retarder
Retarder is an additive used to extend the drying time. Use a small container to hold the retarder as you paint. Apply over an desired area to create a wet-on-wet technique. Use a flat brush with only retarder, keeping it free from water. It will not damage the brush to keep it in retarder over extended periods.

Yellow Glaze Medium
Transparent yellow pigment mixed in a clear glaze medium. This transparent color is chosen for its ability to impart a glowing quality without hazing. Lightly retard painting area and work a little yellow glaze over highlights where desired throughout the piece.

Finishing

Using tack cloth, remove lint, dust, or dirt. Erase any remaining pattern lines.

Choose finishes that are nonyellowing and quick drying. Aerosol varnishes or finishes are convenient and available in gloss, satin, or matte finishes.

On painted surfaces, spray the dry, completed project with a coat of finish. Let dry. Spray a second coat and let dry. Sand surface with wet 400-grit sandpaper. Wipe away all dust. If necessary, apply an additional finish coat.

If project is made of new wood and was stained or glazed, the wood is rather porous. This means the surface will soak up most of the first coat of finish, requiring more coats than a painted surface.

A piece that will be used outdoors will need more finish coats applied periodically throughout the years.

Waterproof exterior acrylics do not need to be varnished.

To achieve a soft finish on large items, apply water-based varnish with a sponge roller. Do not worry about bubbles, with repeated rollings the bubbles will vanish. Roll until varnish is near dry.

Aerosol Finish
Aerosol finishes are sprayed onto painted surfaces to seal and protect against moisture, soil, and dust. They are available in satin, matte, or gloss and dry clear without yellowing.

Water-based Varnish
Water-based varnishes are brushed onto surfaces to seal and protect against moisture, soil, and dust. They come in satin, matte, or gloss finishes. They also offer excellent resistance to scratches and water spotting.

Viola & Ivy Patio Table

Viola & Ivy Patio Table

Materials

Painting Surface:
Birch plywood tabletop,
  36" dia.

Acrylic Paints:
Burnt Carmine (A)
Butter Yellow (D)
Clay Bisque (P)
Dusty Purple (D)
Green Mist (A)
Leprechaun (D)
Light Buttermilk (A)
Light Lime (L)
Rhythm 'n Blue (D)

Brushes:
Filbert, #8
Flats, #6–12
Liner
Round, #3
Scroller, 10/0
Wash, ½", ¾"

Supplies:
Black permanent marker
Exterior satin varnish
Exterior spray paint,
  Taupe
Mist spray bottle
Palette
Palette knife
Retarder
Sandpaper, 220-grit
Sea sponge
Sponge brush, 2"
Sponge roller
Stylus
Tack cloth
Tracing paper
Transfer paper
Wood sealer
Yellow wood stain glaze

Instructions

Preparation:

1. Refer to Surface Preparation on pages 17–18. Prepare tabletop.

2. Spray tabletop with several coats of Taupe.

3. Using spray bottle, mix Green Mist plus water until thin enough to spray. Dampen sea sponge with water and squeeze to remove excess. Spray tabletop with inky Green Mist. Sponge over to soften color. Let dry.

4. Using spray bottle, spray tabletop with inky Clay Bisque. Let dry.

5. Using spray bottle, spray tabletop with inky Light Buttermilk. Let dry.

6. Transfer Viola & Ivy Patio Table Patterns on pages 131–136 onto tabletop.

Viola & Ivy Patio Table
Center Closeup

Paint:

1. Refer to Basic Painting Techniques on pages 12–16.

Viola Flower

1. Refer to Viola Flower Worksheet. Wash some flowers with Dusty Purple and other flowers with Dusty Purple plus Burnt Carmine. Let dry.

2. Randomly wash petals with Rhythm 'n Blue.

3. Transfer individual flower petals from Viola & Ivy Patio Table Patterns onto each flower. Use retarder to shade and highlight.

4. Shade flowers:
1st shade with Dusty Purple
Apply shade color again and
    mop out to soften.
2nd shade with Dusty Purple
    plus Burnt Carmine
Apply shade color again and
    mop out.

5. Highlight flowers:
1st highlight with Clay Bisque
2nd highlight with Light
    Buttermilk

6. Using script liner, add fine lines to three large petals with thinned Burnt Carmine. Paint throat with Butter Yellow plus Light Buttermilk. Paint a tiny one-stroke on each side of yellow throat with Light Buttermilk.

Viola Flower Worksheet

1. Randomly wash viola petals.

2. First shade.

3. First shade mopped out.

4. Second shade; first highlight.

5. Second shade mopped out; second highlight.

6. Paint throat; add lines in the three top petals.

21

Viola Leaf Worksheet

1. Wash and shade leaf.

2. Add secondary veins and highlight leaf.

3. Glaze leaf .

4. Tint and vein leaf.

Viola Leaf & Ivy

1. Refer to Viola Leaf Worksheet and Ivy Worksheet. Wash leaves, stems, and calyx with Green Mist.

2. Shade leaves on left-hand side or bottom and down one side of vein with Leprechaun. Using chisel edge of brush, paint side vein with a float of Leprechaun.

3. Shade stems and calyx with Leprechaun.

4. Highlight leaves, stems, and calyx with Light Lime.

5. Paint scrolls and tendrils among flowers and leaves with thinned Leprechaun.

6. Apply light coat of retarder to leaves, stems, and calyx. Using filbert brush and very little paint, randomly tint areas with Light Lime, Dusty Purple, Burnt Carmine, and yellow stain glaze. Let dry 24 hours.

Finish:

1. Using sponge roller, apply two coats of exterior satin varnish, following manufacturer's instructions.

Ivy Worksheet

1. Wash and shade leaf.

2. Highlight leaf.

3. Glaze leaf.

4. Tint and vein leaf.

Layered Flowers Chair

Materials

Painting Surface:
Wooden chair

Acrylic Paint:
Black (A)

Gouache:
Aqua
Gold Oxide
Green Oxide
Indian Red Oxide
Iridescent Blue
Iridescent Green
Magenta
Napthol Red Light
Pine Green
Prussian Blue Hue
Raw Sienna
Soft Black
Smoked Pearl
Teal
Titanium White
Turner's Yellow
Ultramarine Blue

Brushes:
Filberts, #4–#8
Flats, #4–#12
Round, #3
Scroller, 10/0
Sponge brush, 2"
Wash, ½"

Supplies:
Black permanent marker
Black spray paint
Exterior satin varnish
Palette
Palette knife
Retarder
Stylus
Tracing paper
Transfer paper
Yellow wood stain glaze

Color mixes

dark blue mix = Raw Sienna + Prussian Blue Hue + Ultramarine Blue

light blue mix = Aqua + medium blue mix + Smoked Pearl 1:1:2

medium blue mix = Aqua + dark blue mix 1:1

dark cool green mix = Teal + Raw Sienna 2:1

dark warm green mix = Pine Green + Raw Sienna 3:2

medium green mix = Green Oxide + Raw Sienna 1:1

dark orange mix = dark red mix + dark yellow mix 1:1

medium orange mix = dark yellow mix + medium red mix 1:1

dark red mix = Napthol Red Light + Raw Sienna + Indian Red Oxide 1:1:1

dark red violet mix = Raw Sienna + Magenta 1:2

medium red mix = Raw Sienna + Napthol Red Light 1:1

dark yellow mix = Gold Oxide + Raw Sienna 1:1

medium yellow mix = Raw Sienna + Turner's Yellow 1:1

Note: Get soft shading and highlighting by brushing a light coat of retarder over items after base-coating. It is much easier to apply tints to items, using retarder first. Apply colors, then soften with mop brush.

Instructions

Preparation:

1. Refer to Surface Preparation on pages 17–18. Prepare wooden chair.

2. Spray metal parts of chair with Black spray paint. Apply Black acrylic paint to wooden parts of chair.

3. Transfer Layered Flowers Chair Pattern on page 109 onto wooden chair.

Blue Blossom Worksheet

1. Wash blossom petals.

2. Second wash.

3. Third wash.

4. Add blossom center; outline work.

5. Line petals; dot centers.

Blue Blossom

1. Refer to Blue Blossom Worksheet. Base-coat petals with a wash of medium blue mix. Add Smoked Pearl to medium blue mix. Using filbert brush, stroke petals just slightly smaller in size than first wash. Add more Smoked Pearl to wash. Stroke a few petals to highlight.

2. Loosely outline petals with a mix of medium blue mix plus Titanium White.

3. Stipple centers with medium orange mix.

4. Using scroller tip, dot around center and on petals with Soft Black plus dark blue mix.

Purple Blossom Worksheet

1. Wash blossom petals.

2. Second wash.

3. Third wash.

4. Add blossom center; outline work.

5. Line petals; dot centers.

Purple Blossom

1. Refer to Purple Blossom Worksheet. Combine dark red violet mix plus medium blue mix to make violet mix. Using a filbert, wash petals. Add a little Smoked Pearl and rewash the petals slightly smaller in size.

2. Add a little Titanium White to previous mix and randomly stroke on a few petals to highlight.

Add Titanium White to mix and loosely outline outside petals.

3. Stipple centers with medium yellow mix.

4. Using stylus, dot around center and on petals with Soft Black plus dark blue mix.

Pink Blossom Worksheet

1. Wash blossom petals.

2. Second wash.

3. Highlight and shade petals.

4. Add blossom center; outline work.

Pink Blossom

1. Refer to Pink Blossom Worksheet. Base-coat petals with a wash of medium red mix. Using filbert brush, stroke individual petals with medium red mix plus Smoked Pearl. Add more Smoked Pearl to mix and stroke slightly smaller individual petals.

2. Shade between petals and behind center with a float of medium red mix. Loosely line petals with medium red mix plus Titanium White.

3. Stipple centers with dark orange mix. Stipple top portion of center with medium yellow mix plus Smoked Pearl to highlight.

4. Dot various sized dots around center with dark blue mix plus Soft Black.

5. Outline petals; dot center.

Daffodil Worksheet

1. Base-coat daffodil.

2. Shade daffodil.

3. Dry-brush daffodil highlights.

Paint:
1. Refer to Basic Painting Techniques on pages 12–16.

Daffodil
1. Refer to Daffodil Worksheet. Base-coat flower with medium yellow mix. Shade with dark yellow mix. Highlight with medium yellow mix plus Smoked Pearl. Shade again if necessary to soften.

2. Thinly apply yellow wood stain glaze to brighten. Loosely line daffodil with medium yellow mix plus Titanium White.

3. Stroke center with medium green mix.

4. Glaze daffodil.

5. Strengthen shades. Add center, one-strokes, and line work.

White Blossom Worksheet

1. Wash blossom.

2. Second wash.

3. Third wash.

4. Add blossom center; outline work.

White Blossom

1. Refer to White Blossom Worksheet. Wash petals with medium red mix plus medium blue mix plus a little Smoked Pearl. Using filbert brush, stroke on individual petals. Lighten mix with more Smoked Pearl and stroke slightly smaller individual petals.

2. Add more Smoked Pearl to mix and wash on individual petals as before, except smaller.

3. Add Titanium White to mix and loosely line outside of petals and add lines to inside of petals.

4. Stipple centers with medium yellow mix. Highlight stipple with Titanium White plus medium yellow mix. Shade center with a float of dark yellow mix plus a little dark red mix along bottom and a "C" shape stroke in center. Dot various sized dots around center with Soft Black.

5. Shade blossom center; add dots.

Daisy Worksheet

1. Wash daisy.

2. Second wash.

3. Third wash.

4. Add daisy center; outline work.

Daisy
1. Refer to Daisy Work-sheet. Use same colors as for white blossoms. Using smaller filbert brush, follow the same technique with only one stroke per petal.

2. Stipple centers with medium yellow mix. Highlight centers with medium yellow mix plus Titanium White. Shade bottom of centers with a float of dark yellow mix plus dark red mix. Dot various sized dots around center with dark blue mix plus Soft Black.

5. Shade daisy center; add dots.

Tulip Worksheet

Tulip

1. Refer to Tulip Worksheet. Combine dark red violet mix plus dark blue mix to make purple mix. Make three values by adding Smoked Pearl to mix. Base-coat tulip with darkest value purple mix.

2. Shade tulip with dark red violet mix plus medium blue mix without Smoked Pearl.

3. Highlight tulip by dry-brushing second value purple mix. Add Titanium White to lightest value purple mix and loosely outline tulip.

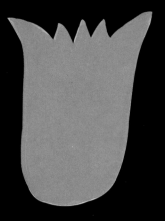

1. Base-coat tulip.

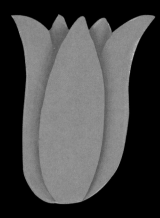

2. Shade tulip.

3. Dry-brush tulip highlights.

4. Add tulip line work.

Tulip & Daffodil Leaf Worksheet

1. Base-coat and
shade leaf.

2. Highlight
leaf.

Tulip & Daffodil Leaves
1. Refer to Tulip & Daffodil Leaf Worksheet. Base-coat leaves with different value greens to add interest. Shade leaves and create vein with a float of the same base color plus a little Soft Black.

2. Highlight leaves and opposite side of vein with base color mix plus a little Smoked Pearl.

3. Tint leaves as desired with any colors used in design. Especially use colors of flowers closest to leaves to tint leaves. Use a little medium yellow mix for sunshine and warmth.

3. Tint leaf.

4. Add lines
and veins.

Rose Worksheet

1. Loosely base-coat rose.

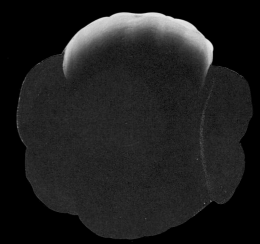

2. Stroke back of rose bowl.

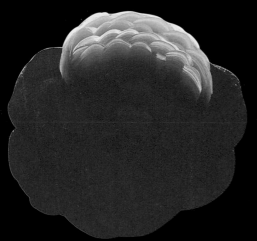

3. Stroke additional petals inside back
of rose bowl.

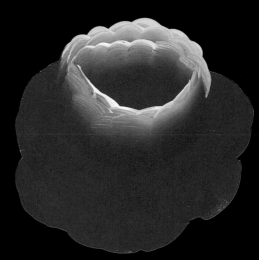

4. Stroke front of rose bowl.

Rose

1. Refer to Rose Worksheet. Loosely base-coat rose with medium red mix.

2. Double-load flat brush with medium red mix and Smoked Pearl. Blend on palette to soften. With Smoked Pearl side of brush at top of rose, stroke on back of rose bowl. Stroke two remaining bowls just slightly inside first one. With Smoked Pearl side of brush at top of rose, stroke on front of bowl. Add two rows of petals to front of bowl slightly below first one. With Smoked Pearl to outside edge, stroke left, right, and center petals.

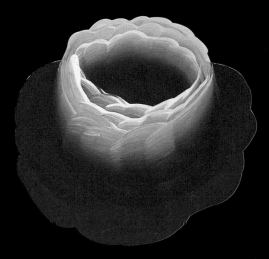

5. Add additional
stroke to rose bowl.

6. Stroke on side and bottom of
rose petals.

7. Shade rose throat and
bottom of bowl.

8. Stroke inside rose petals.
Add stamen dots to center.

3. Shade inside of bowl and outside bottom edge of bowl with dark red mix. Stroke remaining petals to rose with a double load of medium red mix and Smoked Pearl.

4. Dot center with medium green mix and medium yellow mix.

Blossom, Daisy & Rose Leaf Worksheet

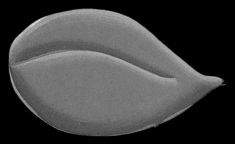

1. Base-coat and shade leaf.

Blossom, Daisy & Rose Leaves
1. Refer to Blossom, Daisy and Rose Leaf Worksheet. Base-coat leaves with different value greens to add interest. Shade leaves and create vein with a float of the same base color plus a little Soft Black.

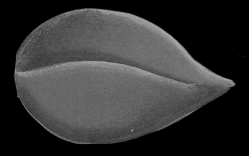

2. Highlight leaf.

2. Highlight leaves and opposite side of vein with base color mix plus a little Smoked Pearl.

3. Tint leaves as desired with any colors used in design. Especially use colors of flowers closest to leaves to tint leaves.

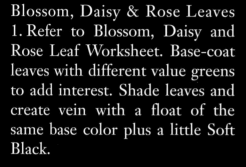

3. Tint leaf.

4. Use a little medium yellow mix for sunshine and warmth.

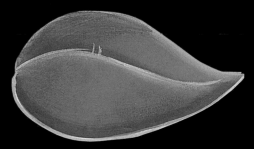

4. Add warmth.

Dragonfly & Bee Worksheet

1. Base-coat
bee; float
wings.

2. Wash wings. Shade
and line body;
highlight head.

3. Add iridescent
color to wings;
vein wings.

1. Base-coat dragonfly;
float wings.

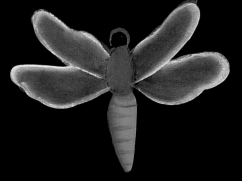

2. Wash wings. Shade and add
detail to body.

3. Add iridescent color to
dragonfly and wings; vein wings.

Dragonfly

1. Refer to Dragonfly & Bee Worksheet. Float wings with Smoked Pearl. Lightly wash center of wings with Smoked Pearl. Add Titanium White to Smoked Pearl to outline wings and line inside of wing.

2. Base-coat head with Soft Black plus a little Titanium White. Add more Titanium White to mix and highlight around head.

3. Base-coat body with medium green mix. Shade with a float of dark cool green mix.

4. Base-coat tail with light blue mix. Shade with a float of dark blue mix and add section lines on tail.

5. Lightly brush body with Iridescent Green and tail with Iridescent Blue. Add iridescent color to wings.

Note: Iridescent colors go a long way, use sparingly.

Bee

1. Float and wash wings with Smoked Pearl. Paint head same as dragonfly.

2. Paint body with medium yellow mix. Shade bottom edge with a float of dark red mix. Make body stripes with Soft Black. Add iridescent color to wings. If retarder was used, let project dry a few days before varnishing.

Finish:

1. Apply two coats of exterior satin varnish, following manufacturer's instructions.

Urn Fountain

Materials

Painting Surface:
Cement ash can with 1" hole
   drilled in center

**Weatherproof, Fade-proof,
   Acrylics:**
Carnation (A)
Chive Green (A)
Daisy Cream (A)
Fiesta Yellow (A)
Honest Copper (A)
Larkspur Blue (A)
Petunia Purple (A)
Pine Green (A)
Sprout Green (A)
Wrought Iron Black (A)

Brushes:
Filberts, #8, #10
Flats, #12, ½", 1"
Liner
Round, #3
Scroller, 10/0
Wash, ½", ¾", 1"

Supplies:
Black permanent marker
Clear flexible tubing, ½"
Fountain pump
Palette
Palette knife
Plastic plumbing 90° elbows, ¾"
Plastic plumbing pipe, ¾",
   12" long
Pond liner
Redwood post, 2' x 4'
River rocks
Sea sponge
Silicone caulking
Sponge roller
Stylus
Tracing paper
Transfer paper

Instructions

Preparation:

1. Refer to Surface Preparation on pages 17–18. Prepare ash can.

2. Using sponge roller, paint ash can with Pine Green until opaque.

3. Wet sea sponge, squeezing out excess water until damp. Lightly sponge Wrought Iron Black on palette to remove excess. Sponge onto ash can, allowing basecoat show through.

4. Using palette knife, mix Pine Green and Larkspur Blue. Sponge color onto ash can. Lightly sponge with Honest Copper. Let dry.

5. Transfer Urn Fountain Pattern on page 130 onto ash can.

Paint:

1. Refer to Basic Painting Techniques on pages 12–16.

Rose

1. Refer to Rose Worksheet on pages 34–35. Loosely base-coat rose with Daisy Cream.

2. Double-load flat brush with Daisy Cream and Pine Green. Blend on palette to soften colors. With Daisy Cream to top portion of rose, stroke on back of bowl. Reload brush as often as necessary and stroke in remaining inside petals. Reload brush and stroke in front portion of bowl. Reload brush as often as necessary and stroke in remaining layers on front of bowl. Reload brush and stroke on side petals and bottom center petal. Let all layers dry.

3. Using 1" flat brush, float inside and bottom of bowl with Pine Green. Stroke on side and bottom petals. Stroke all remaining petals on inside of rose. Smaller roses are painted the same with ½" flat brush.

4. Randomly tint roses and leaves with Carnation. Be certain paint is transparent so as not to lose detail or value. Repeat process with Petunia Purple, then Fiesta Yellow. Randomly edge roses and serration on leaves with Honest Copper.

Rose Leaf Worksheet

1. Base-coat and shade leaf.

2. Highlight leaf.

3. Tint leaf.

4. Strengthen vein lines.

Leaves

1. Refer to Rose Leaf Worksheet. Base-coat leaves with Chive Green.

2. Shade along bottom edge of leaf and down one side of vein with Sprout Green. Using chisel edge of brush, pull secondary veins in leaf.

3. Highlight leaves with Larkspur Blue plus a little Daisy Cream. Using mop brush, highlight leaves and soften edges.

4. Tint leaves as desired with any colors used in design. Especially use flower colors closest to leaves. Use a little yellow stain glaze to add sunshine and warmth.

Stems

1. Paint stems to individual roses and leaves with Larkspur Blue plus Honest Copper. Let dry at least 5 days before running water.

Finish:

1. With outdoor acrylic paints, there is no need to varnish.

Assembly:

1. Slide clear tubing through bottom of ash can up to top so approximately 3" is above bottom of bowl. Seal space between fountain hole and tubing with silicone caulking. Let dry 24 hours.

2. To make a decorative water pattern, insert fountain jet into tubing in bowl. Slide the 90° elbow over tubing on bottom of fountain to prevent tube from bending due to weight of fountain. Slide 12" length of pipe over remaining tube.

There should be enough tubing to hook to the water pump with a little to spare.

3. Make pond for ash can 36" x 36" x 7".

4. Line dirt with pond liner and frame with redwood post. Set pump in hole with some river rocks, set ash can on rocks and fill with remaining rocks.

5. Fill hole with water and turn on pump to highest setting. The water should go through tube up to fountain, fill fountain and overflow to rocks. Fill pond often because of evaporation.

Urn Fountain Closeup

Dramatic Fuchsias Water Fountain

Materials

Painting Surfaces:
Terra-cotta pots 6" (2)
Terra-cotta pot, 8"
Terra-cotta pot,
   4" high x 5"dia.
Terra-cotta saucers, 4" (3)
Terra-cotta saucer, 7½"
Terra-cotta saucer, 8"
Terra-cotta base tray, 21"

Weatherproof, Fade-proof Acrylics:
Burgundy Rose (A)
Carnation (A)
Citrus Green (A)
Cloud White (A)
Fiesta Yellow (A)
Fuchsia (A)
Geranium Red (A)
Pansy Purple (A)
Peach Blossom (A)
Pine Green (A)
Sprout Green (A)
Woodland Brown (A)
Wrought Iron Black (A)

Brushes:
Filbert, #6 or #8
Flats, #4, #6, #8, #12
Liner
Scroller, 10/0
Wash, ½"

Supplies:
Black permanent marker
Drill
Flexible tubing, ½"
Masonry drill bit, ¼"
Palette
Palette knife
Pencil
Rasp
Silicone sealant
Small submersible pump
Stylus
Tracing paper
Transfer paper

Instructions

Preparation:

1. Refer to Surface Preparation on pages 17–18. Prepare pots and saucers.

2. Drill ¼" hole in center of 8" saucer. Using rasp, enlarge holes to ½" to accommodate tubing.

Note: Do not worry if hole is a little larger, because sealer will seal extra space.

3. Rasp four grooves in rim of one 6" pot. Rasp four grooves in one of the 4" saucers. One 4" saucer does not need a groove. Rasp one groove in remaining saucers.

4. Apply two coats of Wrought Iron Black to pots and saucers.

5. Transfer Dramatic Fuchsias Water Fountain Patterns on page 113 onto pots.

Fuchsia Leaf Worksheet

1. Base-coat leaf.

2. Shade leaf; float vein lines.

3. Highlight leaf.

4. Tint leaf; add veins.

Paint:
1. Refer to Basic Painting Techniques on pages 12–16.

Leaves
1. Refer to Fuchsia Leaf Worksheet. Base-coat leaves with Sprout Green until opaque.

2. Shade leaves with Pine Green.

3. Highlight leaves with Cloud White plus Sprout Green.

4. Using #6 filbert brush and very little paint, dry-brush highlights on leaves with Citrus Green.

Fuchsia Flower Worksheet

1. Undercoat fuchsia.

2. Base-coat fuchsia.

3. Shade fuchsia.

4. Highlight fuchsia.

5. Add stamens and lines.

Fuchsia Bud Worksheet

1. Undercoat bud.

2. Base-coat bud.

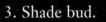

3. Shade bud.

4. Highlight bud.

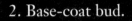

5. Dry-brush bud
highlights
to strengthen.
Highlight shine lines.

Fuchsias

1. Refer to Fuchsia Flower Worksheet on page 45 and Fuchsia Bud Worksheet on page 46. Base-coat flower parts, buds, and stems with Carnation until opaque.

Note: This will be an undercoat for red paints.

2. Base-coat top part of fuchsia, buds, and stems with Geranium Red until opaque.

3. Wash over bottom portion of petals with Fuchsia plus Pansy Purple.

4. Shade on red portion of flowers and buds:
1st shade with Burgundy Rose
2nd shade with Woodland Brown

5. Shade on bottom portion of fuchsia:
1st shade with Fuchsia plus Pansy Purple
2nd shade with Pansy Purple

6. Highlight red portion of fuchsia and stems with Peach Blossom. Highlight bottom portion with Carnation.

7. Using #6 filbert brush and very little paint, dry-brush highlights on buds with Peach Blossom. Using scroller highlight strokes, on buds with Carnation.

8. Paint stamens of fuchsia with Geranium Red. Add daubs of color to ends with Citrus Green. Let dry.

9. Make smaller daubs of paint over green with Fiesta Yellow. Paint little cap ends of fuchsia with Citrus Green shaded with Pine Green.

Finish:

1. There is no need to varnish waterproof exterior paints. Let dry 72 hours.

Assembly:

1. Slide tubing up through inside of 6" pot. Slide 8" saucer over tubing. Seal around edges of saucer and tubing with silicone sealant.

2. Glue two 4" saucers together, bottom to bottom, with silicone. Be certain the saucer with the groove is on top. Set aside to dry, following manufacturer's instructions.

3. Hook tubing to water pump so pump sits at bottom of pot. Set pot assembly at back of 21" base saucer. Be certain pump is covered and electrical cord fits under one groove carved in pot.

4. Place 4" saucer with four grooves upside down to cover the tubing in 8" saucer below. Place 6" potted plant in pot and set atop inverted saucer.

5. Place 4" pot with 7½" saucer on top, below and next to the pot with the pump. The water from the first pot falls into 4" pot.

6. Place the two saucers that are glued together with groove facing up so water from second pot empties into it. Water from small saucers should empty into large base saucer.

7. Add 8" pot with plant in it to any place desired in base tray.

Hydrangeas Silver Birdhouse

Materials

Painting Surfaces:
Funnel, 5"
Rose pot, 6"
Saucer, 6"

Acrylic Paints:
Avocado (A)
Buttermilk (A)
Deep Fuchsia (L)
Deep Periwinkle (A)
Green Forest (P)
Lavender (A)
Lima Green (D)
Rhythm 'n Blue (D)

Gouache:
Pale Gold Metallic
Silver Metallic

Brushes:
Filbert, #8
Flats, #4, #8, #10
Rounds, #3, #5
Scroller, 10/0
Wash, ½"

Supplies:
Black permanent marker
Coupling nut, ¼", 1½" long
Course-thread rod, ¼"
Cutting wheel
Drill
Exterior satin varnish
Gray metal primer
Masonry drill bit, ¼"
Nuts, ¼" (2)
Palette
Palette knife
Pencil
Rasp
Round bead, 1½"
Steel eyebolt, ¼"/20" x 6"
Tracing paper
Transfer paper
Washer, ¼" x 1¼" (2)

Instructions

Preparation:

1. Refer to Surface Preparation on pages 17–18. Prepare surfaces.

2. Apply several coats of metal primer on funnel until well covered. Let dry for 24 hours.

3. Using masonry bit, drill ¼" hole through center of saucer. Drill hole on pot for opening of birdhouse. Using rasp, enlarge hole to 1".

4. Paint pot, saucer, bead, and funnel with a mix of Silver Metallic plus Pale Gold Metallic until opaque.

5. Transfer Hydrangeas Silver Birdhouse Pattern on page 127 onto surfaces.

Paint:

1. Refer to Basic Painting Techniques on pages 12–16.

Lavender Hydrangea
1. Refer to Lavender Hydrangea Worksheet. Paint flower area in slip-slap motion with Buttermilk. While wet, randomly slip-slap Lima Green to create green cast in center.

Note: Work quickly so paint does not dry until achieving desired look. Retransfer flower pattern if necessary.

2. Vary flower colors by floating outside edge of petals with Lavender and Deep Periwinkle. Avoid covering green and cream in center of each petal.

3. Float Rhythm 'n Blue on portions of each flower to vary colors. Float a little Deep Fuchsia for dark shade.

4. Dot centers with Lavender. Shade with a float of Rhythm 'n Blue.

5. Dot around centers with Pale Gold Metallic plus a little Silver Metallic. Pull lines in petals with Pale Gold Metallic.

48

Lavender Hydrangea Worksheet

1. Dry-brush flower.

2. Base-coat hydrangea; first shade.

3. Second shade.

4. Add linework; dot centers.

Lavender Hydrangea Leaf Worksheet

1. Base-coat leaf. Add first shade; highlight and vein lines.

2. Highlight leaf.

3. Strengthen vein lines.

Hydrangea Leaves

1. Refer to Lavender Hydrangea Leaf Worksheet. Base-coat leaves with Avocado until opaque.

2. Shade down one side of vein and bottom edge of leaf with Green Forest. Using chisel edge of brush, float secondary veins with Green Forest.

3. Using #8 filbert brush and very little paint, highlight leaves with Lima Green.

4. Tint leaves with Deep Periwinkle, Lavender, and Rhythm 'n Blue. Vary areas with different colors to add interest.

5. Float bottom of pot, saucer, and behind outside edge of design with Pale Gold Metallic plus a little Silver Metallic. Stroke scrolls on funnel and all bare areas of pot with Pale Gold Metallic.

6. Stroke rim and bottom of funnel with one-strokes of Deep Periwinkle and a smaller one-stroke of Deep Fuchsia in center of larger strokes. Paint small check strokes between one-strokes with Deep Fuchsia.

7. Paint small one-strokes with Lima Green. Paint saucer bottom with same strokes as funnel, using same colors. Let dry 24 hours.

Finish:

1. Apply two coats of exterior satin varnish, following manufacturer's instructions. Let dry.

Assembly:

1. Insert eyebolt through bead and into top of funnel. Slip washer over eyebolt and push up to inside of funnel. Secure tightly in place with nut.

2. Screw coupling nut to end of eyebolt, leaving enough of coupling nut to screw on the ¼" rod. Insert coupling nut and rod through pot, through saucer, add washer, and screw tightly with nut.

3. Using cutting wheel, cut off excess rod as close to nut as possible.

Cone Flowers on Weathered Copper Birdhouse

Materials

Painting Surfaces:
Decorative finial of choice
Funnel, 8"
Rose pot, 6"
Saucers, 4", 8"

Acrylic Paints:
Burnt Carmine (P)
Dusty Plum (P)
Dusty Purple (P)
Green Forest (P)
Pale Yellow (D)
Patina (P)
Rhythm 'n Blue (D)
Salem Green (D)
Summer Sky (P)
Terra Cotta (D)
White (D)

Brushes:
Flats, #4, #6, #8, #12
Round, #5
Scruffy flat, #6

Supplies:
Black permanent marker
Copper metal pigment paint
Copper activator
Coupling nut, ¼" x 1½"
Course-thread screw rod, ¼", 24" long
Cutting wheel
Drill
Exterior satin varnish
Gray metal primer
Masonry drill bits, ⅛", ¼"
Nuts, ¼" (2)
Palette
Palette knife
Rasp
Sea sponge
Steel eyebolt, ¼"/20" x 6"
Stylus
Tracing paper
Transfer paper
Verdigris stone-textured finish
Washers, ¼" x 1¼" (2)

Instructions

Preparation:

1. Refer to Surface Preparation on pages 17–18. Prepare funnel, pot, and saucers.

2. Spray funnel with several light coats of gray metal primer. Let dry 24 hours.

3. Randomly space and drill three ¼" holes in pot. Using rasp, enlarge holes to 1".

4. Drill ¼" hole through center of both saucers. Drill ⅛" pilot hole through center of finial. Using ¼" bit, enlarge hole in finial. Using rasp, enlarge opening in bottom of finial to fit on tube of funnel.

5. Paint pot and both saucers with Patina. Let dry.

6. Spray verdigris stone-textured finish on pot and saucers. Let dry 24 hours.

7. Base-coat 8" saucer, finial, and funnel with at least three coats of copper metal pigment paint.

8. Using sea sponge, apply copper activator to copper areas (not inside on saucer). Set aside until activator turns copper green.

9. Transfer Cone Flowers on Weathered Copper Birdhouse Pattern on page 112 onto project.

Cone Flower Worksheet

1. Base-coat flower, stipple center.

2. First shade.

3. Second shade.

4. First highlight.

5. Second highlight; center highlight.

Paint:
1. Refer to Basic Painting Techniques on pages 12–16.

Cone Flower
1. Refer to Cone Flower Worksheet. Base-coat cone flowers with Dusty Plum until opaque.

2. Shade flowers:
1st shade with Dusty Purple
2nd shade with Rhythm 'n Blue

3. Highlight flowers with Dusty Plum plus White, then with Pale Yellow.

4. Stipple flower centers with Burnt Carmine. Stipple highlights with Terra Cotta.

Cone Flower Leaf Worksheet

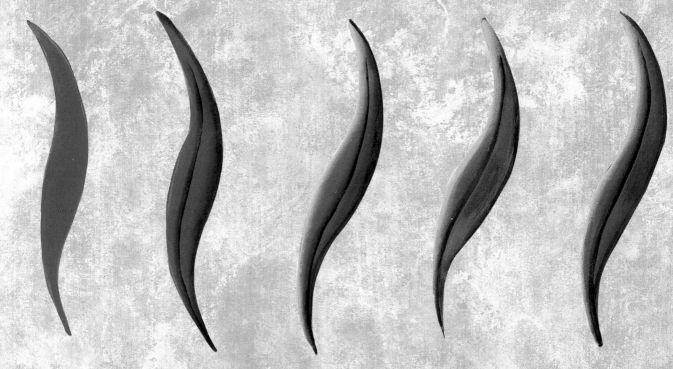

1. Base-coat leaf.
2. Shade leaf.
3. Highlight leaf.
4. Tint leaf.
5. Vein leaf.

Leaves

1. Refer to Cone Flower Leaf Worksheet. Base-coat leaves with Salem Green until opaque.

2. Shade leaves and veins with Green Forest.

3. Highlight leaves with Summer Sky.

4. Tint leaves with Dusty Purple. Using scroller, vein leaf with Green Forest. Let dry 24 hours.

Finish:

1. Apply two coats of exterior stain varnish, following manufacturer's instructions.

Assembly:

1. Insert eyebolt into finial and down through funnel. Slide washer over eyebolt and tighten with nut to secure finial to funnel tightly.

2. Screw half of coupling nut to eyebolt and other half to ¼" rod.

3. Insert rod into pot, down through inverted 4" saucer and into bottom 8" saucer. Slip on washer and tighten with nut to secure saucers, pot, and funnel together.

4. Using cutting wheel, cut off excess rod as close to nut as possible.

Sunflower Stepping Stone

Materials

Painting Surface:
Cement stepping stone, 12"

**Weatherproof, Fade-proof
Acrylic Paints:**
Caramel (P)
Fiesta Yellow (A)
Golden Honey
Larkspur Blue (A)
Limestone (P)
Olive Green (P)
Patio Brick (A)
Pine Green (A)
Sprout Green (A)
Terra Cotta (A)
White (P)
Woodland Brown (A)
Wrought Iron Black (A)
Clear coat (A)

Brushes:
Flats, #4–12
Round, #5
Scroller, 10/0
Scruffy flat, #6
Wash, ½"

Supplies:
Black permanent marker
Palette
Palette knife
Sea sponge
Stylus
Tracing paper
Transfer paper

Instructions

Preparation:
1. Refer to Surface Preparation on pages 17–18. Prepare stepping stone.

2. Base-coat stepping stone with Limestone. Dampen sea sponge, squeeze out excess water, and lightly sponge stepping stone with White, then Caramel, then Olive Green and finally White plus Caramel.

Note: Do not clean sponge between colors. Avoid oversponging, allowing all colors to show.

3. Transfer outside pattern lines only of Sunflower Stepping Stone Pattern on page 118 onto stepping stone.

Paint:
1. Refer to Basic Painting Techniques on pages 12–16.

Leaf
1. Refer to Sunflower Leaf Worksheet. Float both sides of leaves with Sprout Green. Apply heavy wash to inside of leaves.

2. Using fairly dry brush, tint leaves with Fiesta Yellow, a little Larkspur Blue, and Patio Brick by randomly scrubbing color on leaves.

3. Paint scrolls and stems with Sprout Green plus a little Pine Green.

Sunflower Leaf Worksheet

1. Float leaf.   2. Wash leaf.   3. Tint leaf.

Sunflower Worksheet

1. Base-coat; shade.

2. Highlight; line petals. Shade behind and stipple center.

3. Highlight center.

4. Shade around center.

5. Shade center; add various sized dots.

Sunflower

1. Refer to Sunflower Work-sheet. Base-coat sunflower pet-als with Fiesta Yellow.

2. Stipple center with Wood-land Brown.

3. Shade sunflower:
1st shade with Fiesta Yellow plus Golden Honey
2nd shade with Golden Honey

4. Add lines in petals with Golden Honey.

5. Stipple highlight on center with Terra Cotta.

6. Float Patio Brick behind center on petals. Shade center and add various sized dots with Wrought Iron Black.

Finish:

1. With outdoor acrylic paints there is no need to varnish. Apply clear coat for a glossy finish.

Morning Glory Stepping Stone

Materials

Painting Surface:
Cement stepping stone, 12"

Weatherproof, Fade-proof, Acrylic Paints:
Blue Bell (A)
Caramel (P)
Cloud White (A)
Golden Honey (A)
Limestone (P)
Olive Green (P)
Pansy Purple (A)
Pine Green (A)
Sprout Green (A)
Sunflower Yellow (A)
Sunshine Yellow (A)
Tango Blue (A)
Tiger Lily Orange (A)
White (P)
Wrought Iron Black (A)
Clear coat (A)

Brushes:
Flats, #6–12
Liner
Scroller, 10/0
Wash, ½"

Supplies:
Black permanent marker
Palette
Palette knife
Sea sponge
Stylus
Tracing paper
Transfer paper

Instructions

Preparation:

1. Refer to Surface Preparation on pages 17–18. Prepare stepping stone.

2. Base-coat stepping stone with Limestone. Dampen sea sponge, squeeze out excess water and lightly sponge stepping stone with White, then Caramel, then Olive Green, and finally White plus Caramel.

Note: Do not wash sponge between colors. Avoid oversponging, allowing all colors to show.

3. Transfer outside pattern lines only of Morning Glory Stepping Stone Pattern on page 114 onto stepping stone.

Paint:

1. Refer to Basic Painting Techniques on pages 12–16.

Morning Glory Leaves

1. Refer to Morning Glory Leaf Worksheet. Float both sides on leaf and veins with Sprout Green. Apply heavy wash to inside of leaf.

2. Using fairly dry brush, tint leaves with Blue Bell, Pansy Purple, Sunshine Yellow, and Tiger Lily Orange by randomly scrubbing color on leaves.

3. Paint scrolls and stems with Sprout Green plus a little Pine Green.

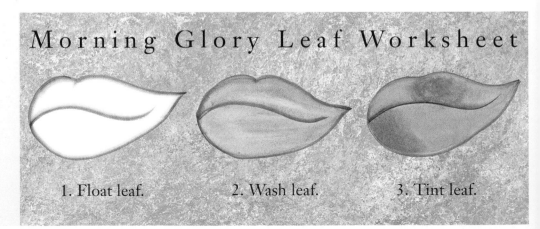

Morning Glory Leaf Worksheet

1. Float leaf. 2. Wash leaf. 3. Tint leaf.

Morning Glory Flower Worksheet

Morning Glories

1. Refer to Morning Glory Flower Worksheet. Base-coat morning glories with Blue Bell plus Cloud White.

2. Transfer Morning Glory Stepping Stone Pattern detail lines onto stepping stone.

3. Shade morning glories:
1st shade with Blue Bell
2nd shade with Blue Bell plus Pansy Purple
3rd shade with Pansy Purple plus Tango Blue

Note: When shading, create small vein lines in petals. If desired, line over veins with White.

4. Paint center stamen with Sunflower Yellow. Shade with Golden Honey. Highlight with Cloud White.

5. Shade throat with Pine Green.

6. Paint calyx with Sprout Green. Shade with Sprout Green plus Wrought Iron Black. Highlight with Sprout Green plus White.

Finish:

1. There is no need to varnish outdoor acrylic paints.

2. For additional gloss, add clear coat to project.

1. Base-coat morning glory; first shade.

2. Second shade.

3. Third shade.

4. Paint; shade; highlight stamen.

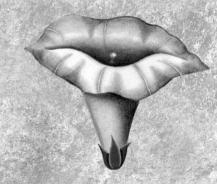

5. Shade throat; highlight vein lines. Add calyx; shade, then highlight.

Poppy Stepping Stone

Materials

Painting Surface:
Cement stepping stone, 12"

Weatherproof, Fade-proof , Acrylics:
Burgundy Rose (A)
Caramel (P)
Limestone (P)
Olive Green (P)
Pansy Purple (A)
Pine Green (A)
Red Pepper (A)
Sprout Green (A)
Sunshine Yellow (A)
Tiger Lily Orange (A)
White (P)
Wrought Iron Black (A)
Clear coat (A)

Brushes:
Flats, #4–12
Scroller, 10/0
Scruffy flat, #6
Wash, ½"

Supplies:
Black permanent marker
Palette
Palette knife
Sea sponge
Stylus
Tracing paper
Transfer paper

Instructions

Preparation:
1. Refer to Surface Preparation on pages 17–18. Prepare stepping stone.

2. Base-coat stepping stone with Limestone.

3. Dampen sea sponge, squeeze out excess water, and lightly sponge stepping stone with White, then Caramel, then Olive Green, and finally White plus Caramel.

Note: Do not clean sponge between colors. Avoid oversponging allowing all colors to show.

4. Transfer outside pattern lines only of Poppy Stepping Stone Pattern on page 117 onto stepping stone.

Paint:
1. Refer to Basic Painting Techniques on pages 12–16.

Leaves
1. Refer to Poppy Leaf Worksheet. Float both sides of leaves and vein with Sprout Green. Apply heavy wash to inside of leaves.

2. Using fairly dry brush, tint leaves with Burgundy Rose, Sunshine Yellow, and Tiger Lily Orange by randomly scrubbing color on leaves.

3. Paint scrolls and stems with Sprout Green plus a little Pine Green.

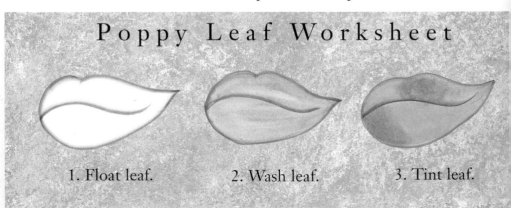

Poppy Leaf Worksheet

1. Float leaf. 2. Wash leaf. 3. Tint leaf.

Poppy Worksheet

1. Base-coat poppy. Transfer pattern. Stipple poppy center.

2. First shade.

3. Second shade.

4. Highlight petals.

5. Highlight center. Add center detail.

Poppy

1. Refer to Poppy Worksheet. Base-coat poppies with Tiger Lily Orange. Stipple centers with Wrought Iron Black.

2. Shade poppies:
1st shade with Red Pepper
2nd shade with Burgundy Rose

3. Highlight poppy petals with Sunshine Yellow plus Tiger Lily Orange.

4. Paint stamens and daub ends with Wrought Iron Black.

5. Stipple highlights on center and add dots on daub ends with Pansy Purple.

Finish:

1. With outdoor acrylic paint, there is no need to varnish. Apply clear coat for a glossier finish.

Wishing Post

Materials

Painting Surface:
Fir post, 4" x 4" x 8'

Acrylic Paints:
Burnt Carmine (P)
Deep Sage (L)
Dusty Khaki (L)
Golden Straw (A)
Green Forest (P)
Lemon Custard (P)
Medium Lavender (L)
Medium Turquoise (L)
Napa Red (A)
Olive Green (A)
School Bus Yellow (P)
True Apricot (L)
True Orange (L)
True Poppy (L)
True Red (L)

Brushes:
Filbert, #6
Flats, #4–12
Liner
Scroller, 10/0
Scruffy flat, #6
Wash, ½"

Supplies:
Black permanent marker
Bombay Mahogany stain
Exterior satin varnish
Palette
Palette knife
Retarder
Sponge brush, 2"
Sponge roller
Stylus
Tracing paper
Transfer paper

Instructions

Preparation:
1. Refer to Surface Preparation on pages 17–18. Prepare post.

2. Using sponge brush, stain post with Bombay Mahogany, following manufacturer's instructions. Let dry 24 hours.

3. Transfer main Wishing Post Patterns lines on pages 124–125 onto post.

Paint:
1. Refer to Basic Painting Techniques on pages 12–16.

Leaves & Buds
1. Refer to Post Poppy Leaf Worksheet and Post Poppy Flower & Bud Worksheet on page 66. Base-coat leaves, stems, and buds with Deep Sage.

2. Transfer leaf detail of Wishing Post Patterns onto post. Shade leaves, stems, and buds with Green Forest.

3. Highlight leaves, stems, and buds with Dusty Khaki plus Deep Sage. Apply light coat of retarder to leaves, stems, and buds.

4. Using filbert brush, randomly tint items with True Poppy, School Bus Yellow, Medium Turquoise, and Olive Green.

Continued on page 67

Post Poppy Leaf Worksheet

1. Base-coat, shade, and highlight.

2. Tint leaf.

3. Vein leaf.

Post Poppy Flower & Bud Worksheet

1. Base-coat poppy. Add first
shade.

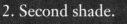

2. Second shade.

1. Base-coat bud.
Add first shade.

3. Third shade.

2. Highlight bud.

4. Highlight; stipple center.

3. Tint bud.

5. Finish center. Restrengthen shades and
highlights as needed.

4. Add linework;
restrengthen
shades.

Continued from page 65

5. Paint fine hairs in darkest areas on stems and buds with Green Forest and in lightest areas with Deep Sage plus Olive Green plus a little Medium Turquoise.

Poppy

1. Refer to Post Poppy Flower & Bud Worksheet. Base-coat poppies with True Orange until opaque.

2. Transfer poppy detail from Wishing Post Patterns onto post.

3. Shade poppy:
1st shade with True Poppy
2nd shade with True Red
3rd shade in darkest recesses with
   Napa Red
4th shade behind center with
   Burnt Carmine

4. Highlight poppy with True Apricot.

5. Using scruffy flat brush, stipple poppy centers:
1st stipple with Medium Lavender
2nd stipple with Golden Straw
   Leave some Medium Lavender
   around outside edges
3rd stipple with Lemon Custard

6. Paint stamens and daub ends with thinned Lemon Custard.

Finish:

1. Using sponge roller, apply two coats of exterior satin varnish, following manufacturer's instructions.

Sweet Pea Rock

Materials

Painting Surface:
Large rock

Acrylic Paints:
Deep Periwinkle (A)
Mint Green (L)
Orchid (A)
Plum (A)
Poetry Green (P)
Portrait Light (P)
Tartan Green (P)
White (D)

Brushes:
Filbert, #6
Flats, #4, #6, #8, #12
Round, #3
Scroller, 10/0
Wash, ½"

Supplies:
Black permanent
    marker
Exterior satin varnish
Palette
Palette knife
Stylus
Tracing paper
Transfer paper
Yellow stain glaze

Instructions

Preparation:
1. Refer to Surface Preparation on pages 17–18. Prepare rock.

2. Transfer Sweet Pea Rock Pattern on page 116 onto rock.

Paint:
1. Refer to Basic Painting Techniques on pages 12–16.

Sweet Pea Leaves
1. Refer to Sweet Pea Leaf Worksheet. Base-coat leaves with Poetry Green until opaque.

2. Shade leaves with Tartan Green. Highlight leaves with Mint Green.

3. Vein leaves with Tartan Green.

4. Randomly tint leaves with a light wash of Deep Periwinkle. Wash over leaves with yellow stain glaze, followed by a little Orchid, then tint leaves with Plum.

Sweet Pea Leaf Worksheet

1. Base-coat and shade leaf.

2. Highlight leaf.

3. Tint leaf.

4. Add veins.

Sweet Pea Worksheet

1. Base-coat sweet pea; first shade.

2. Second shade mopped out.

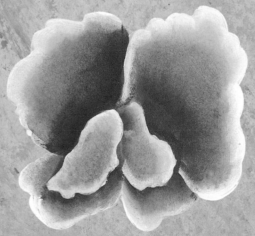

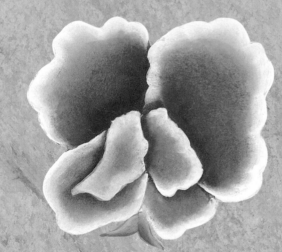

3. Highlight sweet pea.

4. Tint sweet pea; add calyx.

Sweet Pea

1. Refer to Sweet Pea Worksheet. Base-coat sweet peas with Orchid plus White until opaque.

2. Shade sweet peas:
1st shade with Orchid
2nd shade with Plum
    Mop out to soften.
Use retarder when necessary.

3. Highlight sweet peas with Portrait Light.

4. Tint sweet peas with Deep Periwinkle.

5. Base-coat calyx with Poetry Green.

6. Shade calyx with Tartan Green.

7. Highlight calyx with Mint Green.

70

Sweet Pea Pod Worksheet

1. Base-coat pea pod; first shade.

2. Highlight pea pod.

3. Tint pea pod.

4. Add calyx; shade; highlight pea pod.

Pea Pod

1. Refer to Sweet Pea Pod Worksheet. Base-coat pea pods, and calyx with Poetry Green until opaque.

2. Shade calyx, and pea pods with Tartan Green.

3. Highlight calyx, and pea pods with Mint Green.

4. Tint pea pods with a light wash of Deep Periwinkle. Tint leaves and pea pods with Plum. Let dry 24 hours.

Finish:

1. Apply two coats of exterior satin varnish, following manufacturer's instructions.

Chinese Blossom Happiness Rock

Materials

Painting Surface:
Large rock

Acrylic Paints:
Bittersweet Chocolate (A)
Clay Bisque (P)
Deep Coral (A)
Deep Sage (L)
Lisa Pink (D)
Straw (D)
White (D)

Brushes:
Filberts, #6, #8
Liner
Round, #5
Scroller, 10/0

Supplies:
Black permanent marker
Exterior satin varnish
Palette
Palette knife
Stylus
Tracing paper
Transfer paper

Instructions

Preparation:
1. Refer to Surface Preparation on pages 17–18. Prepare rock.

2. Transfer Chinese Blossom Happiness Rock Patterns on pages 110–111 onto rock.

Paint:
1. Refer to Basic Painting Techniques on pages 12–16.

Branches
1. Refer to Branch Worksheet. Using filbert brush, paint large and small branches with Bittersweet Chocolate tipped in Clay Bisque until opaque.

Branch Worksheet

1. Base-coat branch.

Chinese Blossom Happiness Rock
Worksheet

Lisa Pink tipped
in White

Lisa Pink tipped
in Deep Coral

Deep Coral tipped
in Lisa Pink.

Bud

Lettering

Blossoms & Bud

1. Refer to Chinese Blossom Happiness Rock Worksheet. Stroke flower petals from outside to center. Paint some flowers Lisa Pink tipped in White, some Lisa Pink tipped in Deep Coral, and some Deep Coral tipped in Lisa Pink. Stoke bud with Lisa Pink tipped in Deep Coral.

2. Stipple centers with Straw. Stipple White over Straw to soften. Paint stamen lines with Straw, daub ends with Deep Coral. Paint buds with varied flower colors.

Leaves

1. Refer to Branch Worksheet on page 72. Stroke leaves and bud base with Deep Sage. Tip some leaves with Clay Bisque to vary color.

Lettering

1. Free-hand lettering with Bittersweet Chocolate. Let dry 24 hours.

Note: Chinese lettering means Happiness.

Finish:

1. Apply two coats of exterior satin varnish, following manufacturer's instructions.

Gerbera Daisies Candleholders

Materials

Painting Surfaces:
Terra-cotta candleholders (3)

Acrylic Paints:
Antique Maroon (A)
Black (D)
Burnt Carmine (A)
Brandy Wine (A)
Bright Pastel Green (P)
Bright Pink (P)
Lavender (A)
Maroon (D)
Mellow Yellow (D)
Peach Sherbet (A)
Promenade (P)
Purple Lilac (P)
Raspberry Wine (P)
Salem Blue (D)
Sweetheart Pink (P)
White (D)

Brushes:
Flats, #6, #8
Scroller, 10/0
Scruffy flat, #6
Wash, ½"

Supplies:
Black permanent marker
Exterior satin varnish
Palette
Palette knife
Stylus
Tracing paper
Transfer paper

Instructions

Preparation:
1. Refer to Surface Preparation on pages 17–18. Prepare terra-cotta candleholders.

2. Base-coat one candleholder with Mellow Yellow, one with Bright Pastel Green plus White, and one with Salem Blue plus White until opaque.

3. Transfer main Gerbera Daisies Candleholders Pattern lines on page 112 onto candleholders.

4. Base-coat daisy on Salem Blue pot with Purple Lilac plus White.

5. Base-coat daisy on Mellow Yellow pot with Peach Sherbet plus White.

6. Base-coat daisy on Bright Pastel Green pot with Sweetheart Pink plus White.

7. Transfer rest of Gerbera Daisies Candleholders Pattern lines onto candleholders.

Paint:
1. Refer to Basic Painting Techniques on pages 12–16.

Peach Daisy
1. Refer to Gerbera Daisy Worksheet on page 78.
Shade peach daisy:
1st shade with Peach Sherbet
2nd shade in darkest areas with Promenade

2. Highlight with Peach Sherbet plus White. Randomly tint petals with Mellow Yellow.

3. Stipple center with Maroon. Highlight with Peach Sherbet. Shade with Antique Maroon plus a little Black.

Note: Be careful not to lose dark center color.

Purple Daisy
1. Shade purple daisy:
1st shade with Purple Lilac
2nd shade in darkest areas with
   Lavender

2. Highlight with Purple Lilac plus White.

3. Stipple center with Burnt Carmine. Highlight with Lavender. Shade with Burnt Carmine plus a little Black. Be careful not to lose dark center color.

Pink Daisy
1. Shade pink daisy:
1st shade with Sweetheart Pink
2nd shade in darkest areas with
   Bright Pink

2. Highlight with Sweetheart Pink plus White.

3. Stipple center with Raspberry Wine. Highlight with Sweetheart Pink plus Brandy Wine. Shade with Brandy Wine. Be careful not to lose dark center color. Let dry 24 hours.

Finish:
1. Apply two coats of exterior satin varnish, following manufacturer's instructions.

Gerbera Daisies Candleholders

Gerbera Daisy Worksheet

1. Base-coat daisy; first shade.

2. Second shade; vein center of petals.

3. Shade behind daisy center; highlight.
   Tint only the peach daisy.

4. Add daisy center detail.

Fantasy Flowers Candleholders

Materials

Painting Surfaces:
Terra-cotta
  candleholders (3)

Acrylic Paints:
Bahama Purple (D)
Calypso Orange (D)
Cranberry Wine (A)
Dark Goldenrod (D)
Dark Plum (P)
Dusty Green (L)
Gray Plum (P)
Holiday Red (L)
Hunter Green (L)
Lemon Custard (P)
Lemonade (P)
Light Lime (L)
Midnite Green (A)
Rhythm 'n Blue (D)

Brushes:
Flats, #4, #8, #12
Scroller, 10/0

Supplies:
Black permanent
  marker
Exterior satin varnish
Palette
Palette knife
Retarder (optional)
Stylus
Tracing paper
Transfer paper

Instructions

Preparation:

1. Refer to Surface Preparation on pages 17–18. Prepare candleholders.

2. Refer to Basic Painting Techniques on pages 12–16. Using wet-on-wet technique, slip-slap colors, keeping light colors in center and dark colors to outside.

3. Slip-slap one side of candleholder with Hunter Green. Lighten center with Dusty Green.

4. Shade outside edges with Midnite Green. Highlight very center and soften color with Light Lime. If necessary, use retarder. Repeat on remaining sides until entire candleholder is painted.

5. Transfer Fantasy Flowers Candleholders Patterns on pages 137–138 onto painted side of each candleholder.

Paint:

1. Refer to Basic Painting Techniques on pages 12–16.

Leaves for All Flowers

1. Refer to Fantasy Leaf Worksheet. Paint leaves with Light Lime shaded with a float of Dusty Green and highlight with Lemonade.

2. Stroke above berries, stems, veins, scrolls, and dots with a mix of Light Lime plus Dusty Green.

Fantasy Leaf Worksheet

1. Base-coat leaf.   2. Highlight leaf.   3. Vein leaf.

1. Base-coat flower and center. Shade flower.

2. Shade flower center.

3. Dot flower center.

4. Stroke flower petals.

Blue Flowers & Berries

1. Refer to Blue Flower & Berry Worksheet. Base-coat flower circle with Bahama Purple and flower center with Calypso Orange.

2. Shade behind center with a float of Rhythm 'n Blue; shade center with Dark Goldenrod. Dot top with Lemonade and bottom with Cranberry Wine.

3. Using chisel edge of flat brush, stroke on petals with a float of Lemonade.

4. Paint berries with Calypso Orange shaded with a float of Dark Goldenrod. Highlight with Bahama Purple.

1. Base-coat berry.

2. Highlight berry.

3. Add stem and one-strokes on top of berry.

Fantasy Tulip Worksheet

1. Base-coat tulip; shade top.

2. Shade inside petals.

3. Shade where petals overlap.

4. Highlight over shade on top of tulip.

5. Line tulip; add stamens.

Fantasy Tulip

1. Refer to Fantasy Tulip Worksheet. Base-coat tulip with Lemonade.

2. Shade top of tulip and two inside scalloped edges with a float of Holiday Red. Deepen shading where tulip overlays with a float of Cranberry Wine. Highlight top back edge with Calypso Orange.

3. Pull lines in yellow portion with Lemon Custard. Paint berries with Bahama Purple. Highlight with a float of Lemonade.

4. Stroke stamens with Hunter Green. Highlight with Light Lime.

Fantasy Pansy Worksheet

1. Base-coat pansy.

2. First shade.

3. Second shade.

4. Highlight pansy.

Fantasy Pansy

1. Refer to Fantasy Pansy Worksheet. Base-coat top three petals with Lemonade and two remaining petals with Gray Plum.

2. Using chisel edge of brush, shade top three petals with a float of Gray Plum. Highlight top three petals with Lemon Custard. Shade bottom petals with Dark Plum. Highlight with Lemonade. Darken shading where necessary by reapplying shade color.

3. Paint center with Dark Goldenrod. Stroke each side with Lemonade.

4. Pull lines on pansy with Dark Plum. Paint berries with Dark Goldenrod. Highlight with a float of Gray Plum. Let dry 24 hours.

Finish:

1. Using a large flat brush, apply two coats of exterior satin varnish, following manufacturer's instructions.

Hibiscus Planter Box

H i b i s c u s   P l a n t e r   B o x

Materials

Painting Surface:
Wooden planter box

Acrylic Paints:
Forest Green (A)
Green Mist (A)
Lima Green (D)
Limeade (A)
Medium Red (L)
Moon Yellow (A)
Napa Red (A)
Peaches 'n Cream (A)
Spice Pink (A)
True Apricot (L)
True Red (L)
White (D)

Brushes:
Filbert, #10
Flat, #12
Liner
Round, #3
Scroller, 10/0
Wash, ½", ¾", 1"

Supplies:
Black permanent marker
Exterior satin varnish
Palette
Palette knife
Sponge brush
Stylus
Tracing paper
Transfer paper
Wood sealer

Instructions

Preparation:

1. Refer to Surface Preparation on pages 17–18. Prepare wooden planter box.

2. Using sponge brush, apply wood sealer to planter box. Let dry 24 hours.

3. Paint planter box with White until opaque.

4. Transfer Hibiscus Planter Box Pattern on page 115 onto planter box.

Hibiscus Planter Box
Closeup

Hibiscus Leaf Worksheet

1. Base-coat leaf; first shade.
Add veins.

2. Highlight leaf.

3. Tint leaf.

4. Vein leaf.

Paint:

1. Refer to Basic Painting Techniques on pages 12–16.

Leaves

1. Refer to Hibiscus Leaf Worksheet. Base-coat leaves, calyx, and stem with Green Mist until opaque.

2. Shade leaves, vein, and secondary veins with Forest Green.

3. Highlight leaves, calyx, and stems with Limeade.

4. Tint leaves with Medium Red, then tint leaves heavily with Lima Green.

5. Restrengthen any shades or highlights as necessary on leaves. Lightly vein leaves with Green Mist plus White.

Hibiscus Worksheet

1. Base-coat hibiscus; first shade.

2. Second shade.

3. First highlight.

4. Second highlight.

5. Tint hibiscus petals.

6. Restrengthen shades and highlights as necessary. Add stamen and dots.

Hibiscus

1. Refer to Hibiscus Worksheet. Base-coat flowers with Medium Red until opaque.

Note: To shade, highlight, and tint flowers, apply a light coat of retarder over flower. Using #8 filbert brush, stroke on a small amount of paint. Using mop brush, mop out to soften.

2. Shade flowers:
1st shade with True Red
2nd shade in deepest recesses with Napa Red

3. Highlight flowers:
1st highlight with Spice Pink
2nd highlight with True Apricot

4. Tint flowers heavily with Peaches 'n Cream.

5. Restrengthen any shades or highlights as necessary on flowers.

6. Base-coat stamen with True Red. Add several lines from stamen with True Red.

7. Shade behind stamen with Napa Red. Add five or six medium-sized daubs to top of stamens with Napa Red. Highlight stamen with Spice Pink.

8. Daub ends of remaining stamens with Moon Yellow. Let dry 24 hours.

Finish:

1. Apply two coats of exterior satin varnish, following manufacturer's instructions.

Tulips & Gay Feather
Planter Box

Materials

Painting Surface:
Wooden planter box

Acrylic Paints:
Ballet Pink (P)
Black (D)
Burnt Carmine (A)
Buttermilk (A)
Cadmium Orange (A)
Deep Midnight Blue (A)
Deep Periwinkle (A)
Deep Sage (L)
Dusty Plum (D)
Dusty Purple (D)
Evergreen (A)
Hauser Medium Green (A)
Holiday Red (L)
Ice Storm (D)
Light Buttermilk (A)
Light Lime (L)
Light Yellow (L)
Magenta (D)
Napa Red (A)
Royal Fuchsia (A)
Tangerine (A)
True Apricot (L)
True Orange (L)
Violet Ice (D)
White (D)
Wisteria (D)

Brushes:
Filberts, #8, #10
Flats, #8–12
Liner, #1
Round, #3
Wash, ½", ¾", 1"

Supplies:
Black permanent marker
Exterior satin varnish
Palette
Palette knife
Retarder
Sandpaper, 220-grit
Sponge roller
Stylus
Tack cloth
Tracing paper
Transfer paper
Yellow wood stain glaze

Instructions

Preparation:
1. Refer to Surface Preparation on pages 17–18. Prepare wooden planter.

2. Using large flat brush and wet-on-wet technique, base-coat one side of box with Deep Midnight Blue. Keeping blue in center, pick up Black and work into outside edges, blending where colors meet. Repeat for remaining sides. Use retarder if necessary.

3. Transfer tulips and leaves from Tulips & Gay Feather Planter Box Pattern on pages 128–129 onto planter box.

Tulips & Gay Feather
Planter Box
Closeup

Pastel Tulip Worksheet

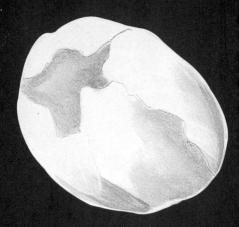

1. Base-coat tulip; first shade.

2. Second shade.

3. First highlight.

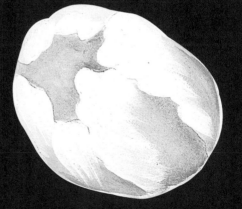

4. Second highlight.

5. Tint petals.

Paint:
1. Refer to Basic Painting Techniques on pages 12–16.

Pastel Tulip
1. Refer to Pastel Tulip Worksheet. Base-coat tulips with Buttermilk until opaque. Apply light coat of retarder when necessary while shading and highlighting.

2. Shade pastel tulips:
1st shade with Wisteria
2nd shade with Deep Periwinkle

3. Highlight pastel tulips:
1st highlight with Violet Ice
2nd highlight with White

4. Tint pastel tulips with Light Yellow, followed by Ballet Pink.

Orange Tulip Worksheet

1. Base-coat tulip; first shade.

2. Second shade.

3. Third shade; first highlight.

4. Second highlight;
add yellow stain glaze.

Orange Tulip

1. Refer to Orange Tulip Worksheet. Base-coat orange tulips with True Orange until opaque. Apply light coat of retarder when necessary while shading and highlighting.

2. Shade orange tulips:
1st shade with Cadmium Orange
2nd shade with Holiday Red
3rd shade with Napa Red

3. Highlight orange tulips:
1st highlight with Tangerine
2nd highlight with True Apricot

4. Tint orange tulips with yellow wood stain glaze.

5. Base-coat tulip centers with True Apricot. Highlight centers with Light Buttermilk.

6. Paint stamen ovals in center with Burnt Carmine.

7. Paint stems from centers to oval stamens with Light Buttermilk plus True Apricot.

5. Strengthen shades and
highlights. Finish tulip center.

Tulip Leaf Worksheet

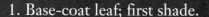

1. Base-coat leaf; first shade.

2. Second shade.

3. First highlight; add yellow wood stain glaze.

4. Restrengthen shades and highlights.

Tulip Leaf

1. Base-coat leaves and stems with Hauser Medium Green until opaque.

2. Shade leaves:
1st shade with Deep Sage
2nd shade with Evergreen

3. Highlight leaves with Light Lime.

4. Tint leaves with yellow wood stain glaze, followed by Cadmium Orange, then Holiday Red.

5. Apply tint colors to leaf.

Gay Feather Worksheet

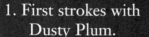

1. First strokes with
   Dusty Plum.

Gay Feather

1. Refer to Tulips & Gay Feather Planter Box Closeup on page 60. Transfer feather from Tulips & Gay Feather Planter Box Pattern on pages 128–129 onto planter.

2. Using round brush, paint flower with a one-stroke. Some strokes are one color, while others are tipped in other colors. Do not clean brush between colors or strokes:
   1st stroke with Dusty Plum
   2nd stroke with Magenta
   3rd stroke with Royal Fuchsia

3. Highlight with Ice Storm plus Royal Fuchsia.

4. Base-coat stems with Dusty Plum plus Dusty Purple. Let dry 24 hours.

Finish:

1. Using sponge roller, apply two coats of exterior satin varnish, following manufacturer's instructions.

2. Second strokes with
   Magenta.

3. Third strokes with
   Royal Fuchsia.

4. Highlight.

Hydrangeas Tile Planter

Materials

Painting Surface:
Square plastic pot, 12" x
    12" opening, 11½" high

Acrylic Paints:
Avocado (A)
Dark Plum (P)
Deep Sage (L)
Evergreen (A)
Gray Plum (P)
Green Forest (P)
Light Lime (L)
Light Yellow (D)
Lima Green (D)
Medium Turquoise (L)
Olive Green (A)
Patina (P)
Rhythm 'n Blue (D)
Winter Blue (A)

Brushes:
Filberts, #8, #10
Flats, #8–#12
Liner
Wash, ½", ¾", 1"

Supplies:
Black permanent marker
Bonding spray for plastic
Exterior satin varnish
Palette
Palette knife
Pencil
Retarder
Ruler
Spray paint, Light Tan
Stylus
Tracing paper
Transfer paper

Instructions

Preparation:

1. Refer to Surface Preparation on pages 17–18. Prepare plastic pot.

2. Apply 2–3 light coats of bonding spray, following manufacturer's instructions. Let dry 24 hours.

3. Spray plastic pot with Light Tan. Let dry 24 hours.

4. Using wet-on-wet technique and working quickly, randomly slip-slap bottom of pot where flowers will be placed with Deep Sage, Evergreen, Green Forest, Light Lime, Medium Turquoise, and Olive Green. Soften colors into each other.

Note: Do not worry about brush strokes showing.

5. Refer to Hydrangeas on Tile Planter Closeup. Using ruler and pencil, mark four square tiles at top of pot.

6. Using wet-on-wet technique, slip-slap paint on first tile with Green Forest and Light Lime. Paint second tile with Medium Turquoise and Olive Green. Paint third tile with Olive Green and Green Forest. Paint fourth tile with Olive Green, Deep Sage, and Medium Turquoise. Repeat painting tiles on remaining side of planter.

7. Transfer Hydrangeas Tile Planter Pattern on page 126 onto pot.

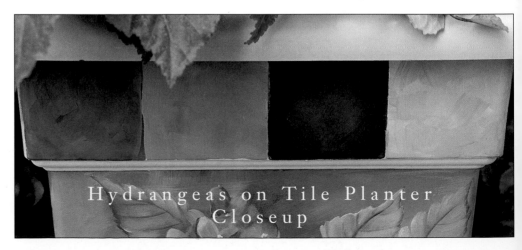

Hydrangeas on Tile Planter
Closeup

1. Base-coat flower; give a
suggestion of petals.

2. Shade flower.

3. Dot flower center. Highlight petals.

Paint:
1. Refer to Basic Painting Techniques on pages 12–16.

Hydrangea
1. Refer to Blue Hydrangea Worksheet. Slip-slap background behind flowers with Dark Plum and Rhythm 'n Blue. Make some flowers more prominent than others to give suggestion of petals. Using dirty brush, pick up additional colors to vary petals. For example, load #8 filbert brush with Gray Plum and tip in Patina, then Gray Plum tipped in Winter Blue, then Gray Plum tipped in Lima Green.

2. After petals are stroked in, float some of the same colors above to add more color on petals. Shade behind some petals with Rhythm 'n Blue to define them from back flowers.

3. Daub centers with Light Yellow. Let dry 24 hours.

Blue Hydrangea Leaf Worksheet

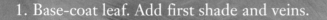

1. Base-coat leaf. Add first shade and veins.

2. Highlight leaf.

3. Tint leaf.

4. Highlight veins.

Leaves

1. Refer to Blue Hydrangea Leaf Worksheet. Base-coat leaves with Avocado.

2. Shade leaves, and center vein with Evergreen. Using chisel edge of brush, stroke secondary veins with Evergreen.

3. Lightly retard leaves. Using #6 filbert brush and very little paint, tint leaves with any colors used on the flower, Lima Green, and Patina. Pull color in from outside edges.

4. Base-coat stems with Avocado. Shade with Evergreen. Highlight with Patina.

Finish:

1. Apply two coats of exterior satin varnish, following manufacturer's instructions.

Hummingbird & Trumpet Vine Watering Can

Materials

Painting Surface:
Galvanized water can

Acrylic Paints:
Buttermilk (A)
Chocolate Cherry (D)
Cranberry Wine (A)
Fruit Punch (D)
Golden Straw (A)
Green Mist (A)
Hauser Dark Green (A)
Iridescent Green (J)
Iridescent Red (J)
Lamp Black (A)
Poppy Orange (D)
Santa Red (A)
Tangelo Orange (A)
Titanium White (A)

Brushes:
Flats, #4–12
Liner
Round, #3
Scroller, 10/0
Wash, ½"

Supplies:
Black permanent marker
Exterior satin varnish
Palette
Palette knife
Retarder
Stylus
Tracing paper
Transfer paper
Yellow wood stain glaze

Instructions

Preparation:
1. Refer to Surface Preparation on pages 17–18. Prepare water can.

2. Transfer Hummingbird & Trumpet Vine Water Can Patterns on pages 119–121 onto water can.

Paint:
1. Refer to Basic Painting Techniques on pages 12–16.

Leaves
1. Refer to Trumpet Vine Leaf Worksheet. Base-coat leaves with Green Mist.

2. Double-load flat brush with Green Mist and Hauser Dark Green. With darker green to outside, stroke on both sides of leaves. Float one side of vein with Hauser Dark Green.

3. Apply retarder to several leaves at a time. Randomly add tints of yellow wood stain glaze, Golden Straw, and Fruit Punch plus Poppy Orange.

4. Pull thin line through vein with Green Mist plus a little Titanium White.

5. Paint calyx, stems, and tendrils with Dark Hauser Green. Highlight calyx with Green Mist. Let dry.

Trumpet Vine Leaf Worksheet

1. Base-coat. 2. Shade. 3. Vein. 4. Highlight vein and tint.

Hummingbird Worksheet

1. Base-coat hummingbird.

2. Add fine strokes to hummingbird. Stroke on front wing feathers.

3. Shade hummingbird. Add linework to tail and beak

4. Glaze hummingbird. Stroke breast over wing.

5. Detail eye. Add iridescent color

Hummingbird

1. Refer to Hummingbird Worksheet. Base-coat tail feather and beak with Lamp Black; throat with Santa Red; tummy with Buttermilk; head, back, back wing, and top of front wing with Hauser Dark Green.

2. Using scroller and thinned paint, stroke fine lines on back and head with Green Mist. Paint throat lines with Tangelo Orange and chest lines with Titanium White.

3. Using round brush, stroke front wing feathers with Green Mist plus Titanium White. Stroke feathers on bottom wing with Titanium White plus a little Green Mist.

4. Float along bottom half of head, behind cheek, above bottom wing, and below bottom wing on back with Lamp Black.

5. Line between tail feathers and beak with Lamp Black plus Titanium White. Dot nostril mark with Lamp Black plus Titanium White for dark gray.

6. Wash over head, back, and front wing with yellow wood stain glaze.

7. Dot eye with Lamp Black, highlight with Titanium White.

8. Pull some Titanium White strokes from breast onto wings to connect with body.

9. Paint head, back, and both wings with Iridescent Green.

10. Paint throat area with Iridescent Red.

Note: If it stands out too much, wash with a little Santa Red to soften. Highlight cheek with tiny stroke of Titanium White.

Trumpet Vine Worksheet

1. Base-coat and glaze.

2. Shade.

3. Highlight.

4. Float lighter highlights;
add calyx

5. Add center. Shade and
highlight calyx.

Trumpet Vine

1. Refer to Trumpet Vine Worksheet. Base-coat flowers with Fruit Punch plus Poppy Orange.

2. Wash yellow wood stain glaze over entire flower.

3. Transfer main lines of Hummingbird & Trumpet Vine Watering Can Patterns onto watering can.

4. Shade with Cranberry Wine. Deepen shading in throat with Chocolate Cherry. Build up shading gradually.

5. Highlight with Tangelo Orange. Float lighter highlights on flower with flower mix plus Buttermilk. Strengthen shades and highlights where necessary.

6. Paint calyx with Dark Hauser Green. Highlight with Green Mist. Let dry.

7. Paint small stamen daubs inside throat of some flowers with thinned Golden Straw.

Finish:

1. Apply two coats of exterior satin varnish, following manufacturer's instructions.

Zinnias Wheelbarrow

Materials

Painting Surface:
Old weathered wheelbarrow

Acrylic Paints:
Alizarin Crimson (A)
Antique Gold (A)
Avocado (A)
Baby Pink (A)
Berry Red (A)
Black (D)
Boysenberry Pink (A)
Butter Yellow (D)
Cadmium Orange (A)
Country Blue (A)
Dioxazine Purple (A)
Light Buttermilk (A)
Marigold (D)
Napa Red (A)
Pumpkin (A)
Red Violet (A)
True Apricot (L)
True Orange (L)
White (D)

Brushes:
Filberts, #6, #8
Flats, #10, #12
Liner
Round, #3
Scruffy flat, #6

Supplies:
Black permanent marker
Exterior satin varnish
Palette
Palette knife
Sponge brush
Stylus
Tracing paper
Transfer paper
Wood sealer

Instructions

Preparation:
1. Refer to Surface Preparation on pages 17–18. Prepare wheelbarrow.

2. Using sponge brush, apply wood sealer, following manufacturer's instructions. Let dry 24 hours.

3. Transfer Zinnias Wheelbarrow Pattern on pages 122–123 onto wheelbarrow.

Flower colors:
gold flower=Antique Gold, Marigold, Butter Yellow, Light Buttermilk
orange flower=Cadmium Orange, Pumpkin, True Apricot, Light Buttermilk
pink flower=Alizarin Crimson, Boysenberry Pink, Baby Pink, Light Buttermilk
purple flower=Red Violet, Dioxazine Purple, Country Blue, Light Buttermilk
red flower=Napa Red, Berry Red, Cadmium Orange, True Orange

Paint:
1. Refer to Basic Painting Techniques on pages 12–16.

Zinnia
1. Refer to Zinnia Worksheet. Load #8 filbert brush in darkest color and tip in next value of color. Pull petals from bottom working up. Use a well-loaded brush and reload often. Lighten color for each row of the flower.

Example: First row: load Napa Red tipped in Berry Red. Second row: load Berry Red tipped in Cadmium Orange. Third row: load Cadmium Orange tipped in True Orange. Buds are painted the same; except, start from top and work to calyx.

Zinnia Worksheet

1. Stroke first row of zinnia.

2. Stroke second row of zinnia.

3. Stroke third row of zinnia; stipple center.

4. Highlight zinnia center.

5. Shade zinnia center; add dots.

Sample of zinnia bud.

Zinnia Centers

Note: Make all centers the same regardless of flower color.

1. Shade behind centers with a float of darkest color of each flower.

2. Stipple centers with Butter Yellow.

3. Highlight centers by lightly stippling with Light Buttermilk.

4. Shade centers with Avocado.

5. Load liner with inky Light Buttermilk. Randomly dot around flower centers, then dot with Avocado plus Light Buttermilk.

Leaves

1. Refer to Zinnia Leaf Worksheet. Base-coat leaves, stems, and calyx with Avocado until opaque.

2. Shade leaves, stems, and calyx with Avocado plus Black. Float veins in leaves.

3. Highlight leaves, stems, and calyx with Avocado plus White. Highlight veins in leaves. Let dry 24 hours.

Finish:

1. Apply two coats of exterior satin varnish, following manufacturer's instructions.

Zinnia Leaf Worksheet

1. Base-coat leaf.

2. Shade leaf and vein.

3. Highlight leaf.

Layered Flowers
Chair Pattern
pages 24-37

Enlarge pattern 160%

Chinese
Blossom
Happiness
Rock Pattern
pages 72–74

Pattern is actual size

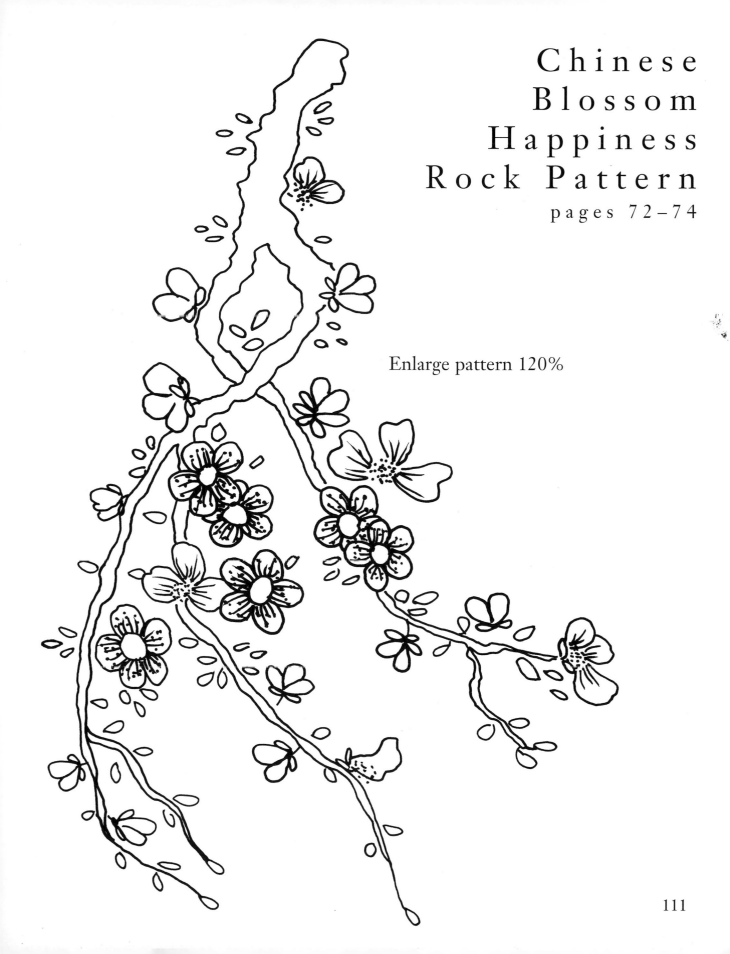

Chinese
Blossom
Happiness
Rock Pattern
pages 72–74

Enlarge pattern 120%

Gerbera Daisies Candleholders Pattern

pages 75–78

Cone Flowers on Weathered Copper Birdhouse Pattern

pages 52–55

Patterns are actual size

Pattern is actual size
for 4" pot

Dramatic
Fuchsias
Water
Fountain
Patterns
pages 42–47

Pattern is actual size
for 6" pot

Enlarge pattern 140%
for 8" pot

Morning Glory Stepping Stone Pattern

pages 59–61

Enlarge pattern 125%

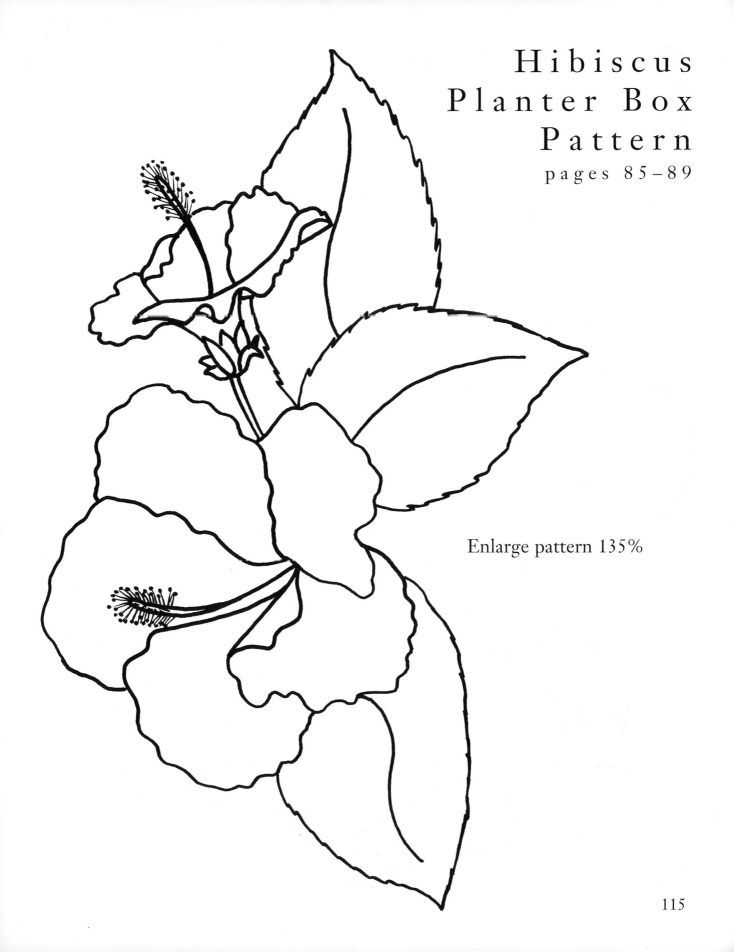

Hibiscus
Planter Box
Pattern
pages 85-89

Enlarge pattern 135%

115

Sweet Pea
Rock Pattern
pages 68–71

Enlarge pattern 115%

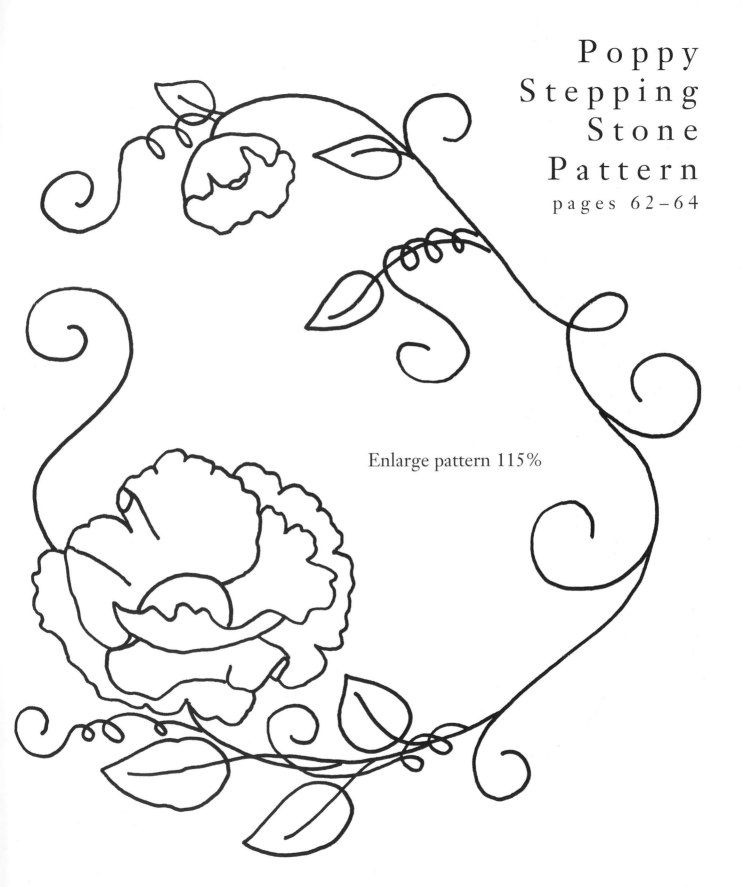

Poppy
Stepping
Stone
Pattern
pages 62–64

Enlarge pattern 115%

Sunflower
Stepping Stone
Pattern
pages 56–58

Enlarge pattern 125%

pages 100–104

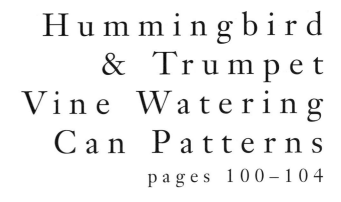

Patterns are actual size

Hummingbird
& Trumpet
Vine Water
Can Pattern
pages 100–104

Pattern is actual size

Hummingbird
& Trumpet
Vine Water
Can Pattern
pages 100–104

Pattern is actual size

Zinnias
Wheelbarrow
Pattern
pages 105–108

Enlarge pattern 125%

Wishing Post
Patterns
pages 65–67

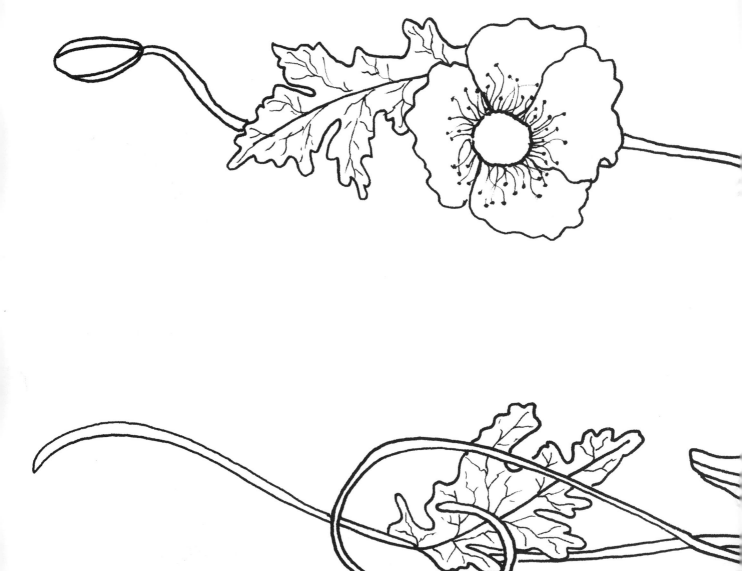

Enlarge patterns 150%

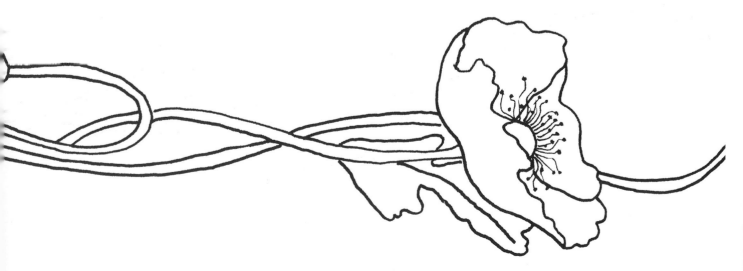

Hydrangeas Tile
Planter Pattern

pages 96–99

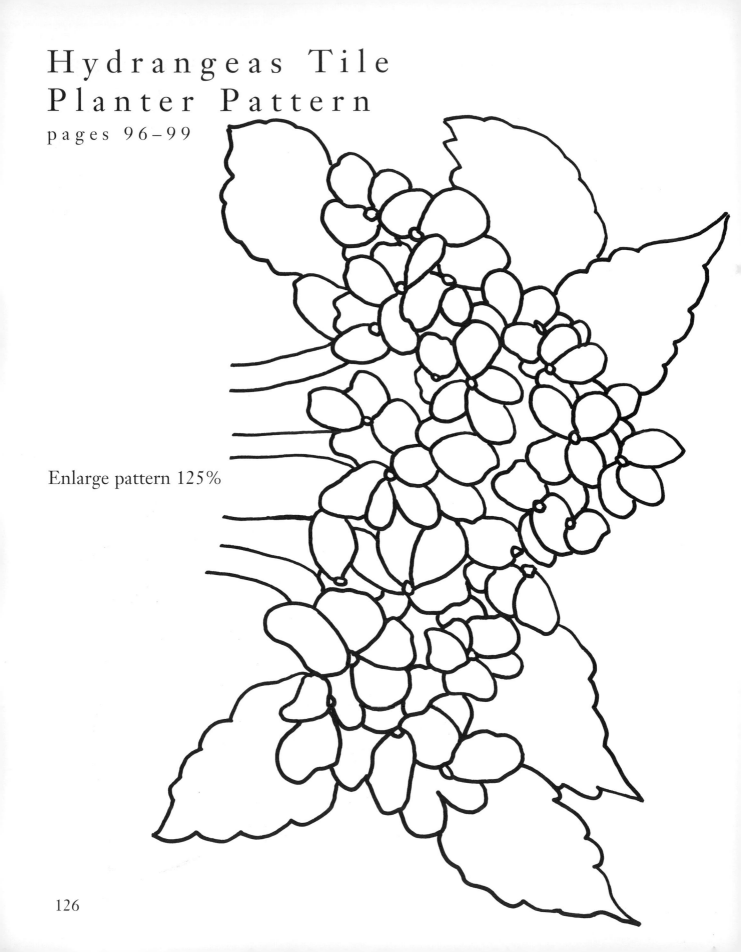

Enlarge pattern 125%

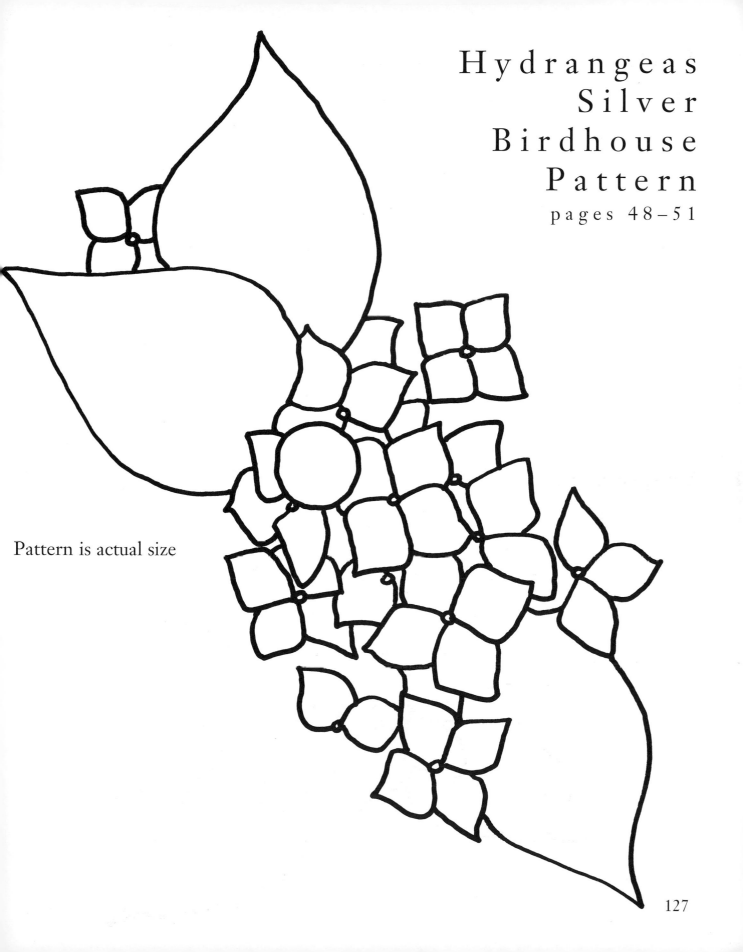

Hydrangeas
Silver
Birdhouse
Pattern
pages 48–51

Pattern is actual size

Tulips & Gay Feather
Planter Box Pattern
pages 90–95

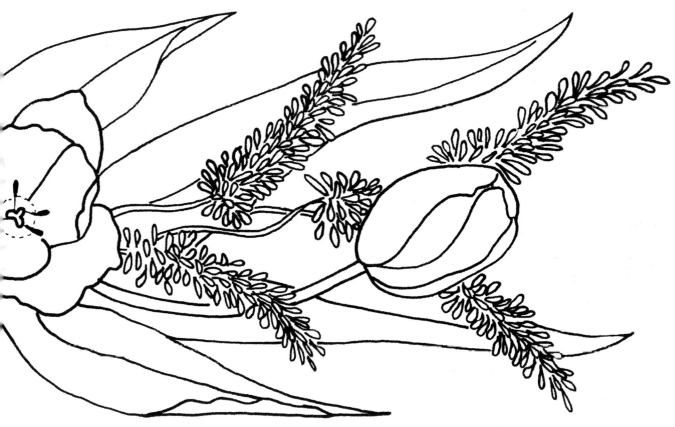

Enlarge pattern 160%

Urn
Fountain
Pattern

pages
38–41

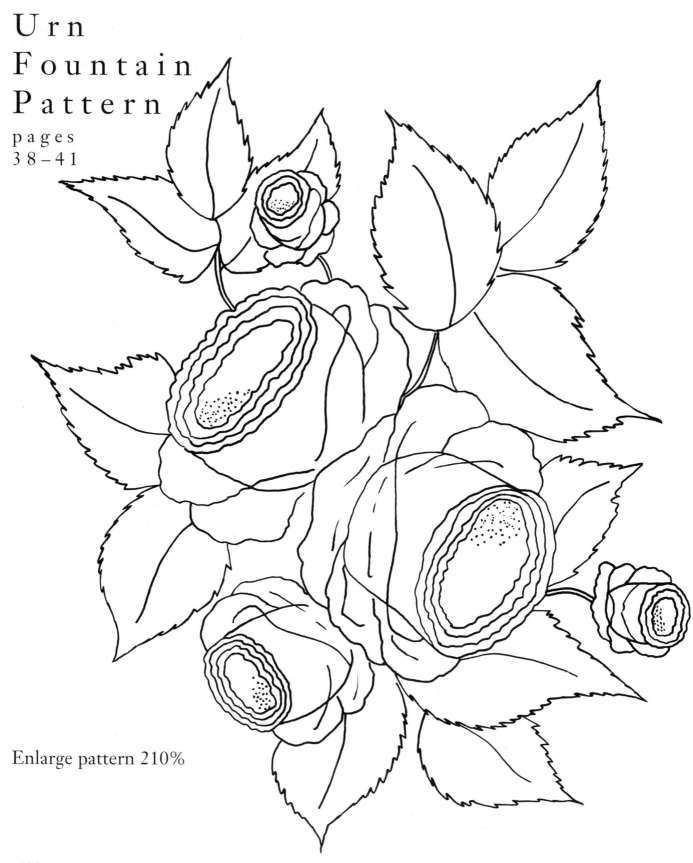

Enlarge pattern 210%

Viola & Ivy Patio Table Pattern

pages 19–23

Pattern is actual size

Viola & Ivy
Patio Table
Pattern

pages 19–23

Pattern is actual size

Viola & Ivy
Patio Table
Pattern
pages 19–23

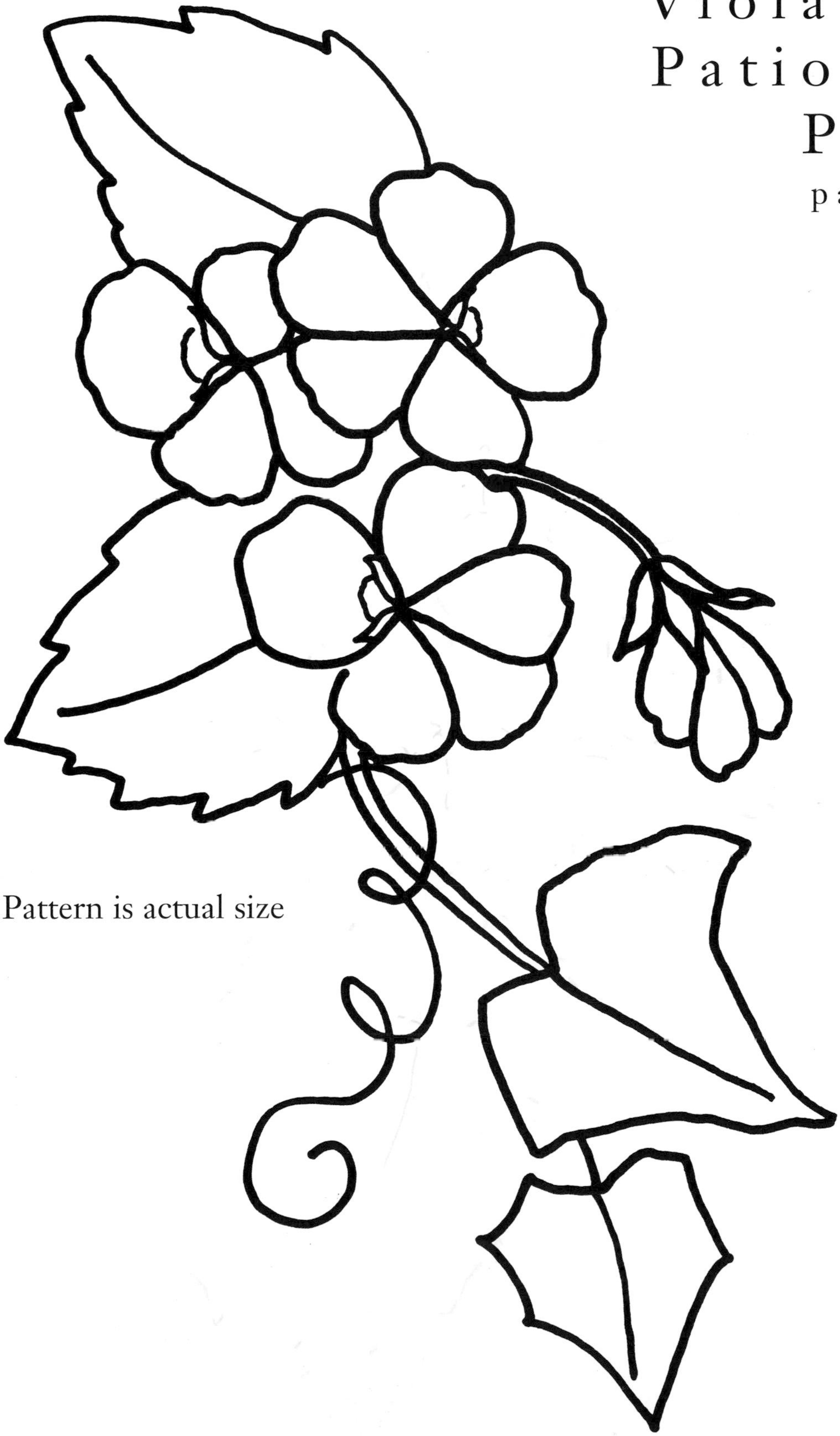

Pattern is actual size

133

Viola & Ivy
Patio Table
Pattern
pages 19–23

Enlarge pattern 145%

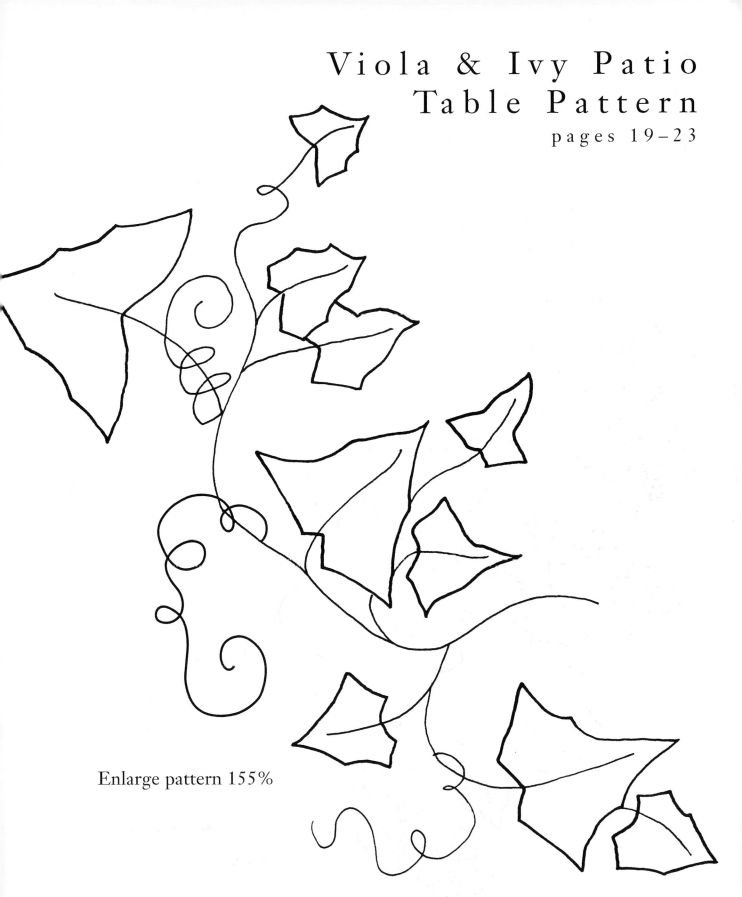

Enlarge pattern 155%

Viola & Ivy Patio Table Pattern

pages 19–23

Enlarge pattern 225%

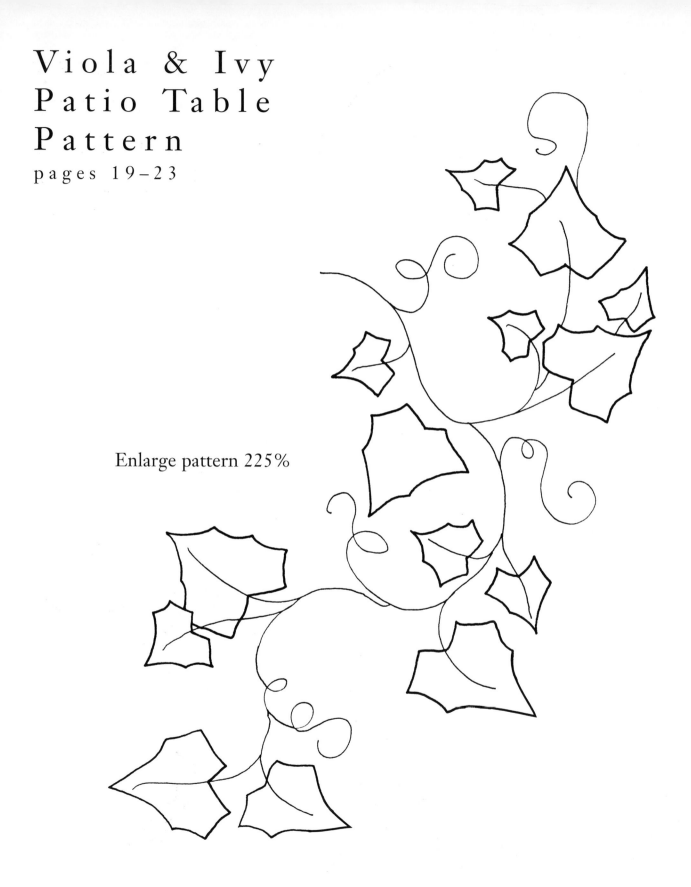

Fantasy
Flowers
Candleholders
Patterns
pages 79–84

Patterns are actual size

Fantasy Flowers
Candleholders
Pattern
pages 79–84

Pattern is actual size

Paint Conversion Chart

Plaid (P)	Delta (D)	Americana (A)	Aleene (L)
Ballet Pink	Pink Quartz + White 2:1	White + Raspberry 4:1	White + True Red (T)
Bright Pastel Green	Spring Green + White	White + Dk Pine	Holiday Green + White
Burnt Carmine	Sweetheart Blush + Candy Bar 3:1	Black Plum	Deep Fuchsia + Burnt Umber
Chocolate Cherry	Candy Bar Brown	Antique Maroon	True Red + Burnt Umber
Clay Bisque	Sandstone	Desert Sand	Beige + Med Gray
Dk Plum	Lavender + Hippo Grey 2:1	Royal Purple + Neutral Grey	Deep Violet + Dusty Gray
Gray Plum	Lavender + Cadet Grey	Pansy Lavender + Ice Blue	True Gray + Dusty Violet + White
Green Forest	Christmas Green	Leaf Green	Deep Green + Hunter Green
Lavender	Purple + White 2:1	Lavender	Deep Violet + White
Lemon Custard	Luscious Lemon	Lemon Yellow	Medium Yellow
Lemonade	Custard	Taffy Cream	Light Yellow
Magenta	Fuchsia	Royal Fuchsia	True Fuchsia
Patina	Turquoise	Sea Aqua + Bluegrass 5:1	True Turquoise + Med Gray + White
Poetry Green	Green Sea + Rainforest (T)	Green Mist	Dusty Green + White
Portrait Light	White + Napthol Red Light 15:1	Hi-Lite Flesh	White + Lt Poppy (T)
Promenade	Coral + Rosetta	Shading Flesh + White	Deep Blush + White
Purple Lilac	Lavender	Lavender + Neutral Grey 3:1	Dusty Violet + White
Raspberry Wine	Sonoma	Cranberry Wine	Deep Fuchsia + Burnt Umber
School Bus Yellow	Yellow	Primary Yellow	True Apricot + White
Summer Sky	Blue Wisp	Blue Mist	Deep Spruce + Dusty Gray + White
Sweetheart Pink	Lisa Pink	Spice Pink + White	White + Holiday Red
Tartan Green	Woodland Night	Deep Teal	Dusty Green

Delta (D)	Plaid (P)	Americana (A)	Aleene (L)
Bahama Purple	Lt Periwinkle + Lavender 4:1	Deep Periwinkle	Med Lavender
Butter Yellow	Buttercup	Moon Yellow	Yellow Ochre + True Yellow
Calypso Orange	Tangerine + White 4:1	Tangerine + Moon Yellow 2:1	Med Apricot
Dk Goldenrod	Butterscotch	Tangerine + Terra Cotta 2:1	True Orange + Burnt Umber
Deep Coral	Primrose	Boysenberry + Crimson Tide 3:1	True Red + White
Dusty Plum	Vanilla Cream + Plum Pudding 3:1	Mauve + Taupe 2:1	Med Violet + True Gray
Fruit Punch	Christmas Red	Cadmium Red	Holiday Red
Ice Storm	Gray Mist + Orchid 10:1	Grey Sky + Orchid 2:1	White + Dusty Violet (T)
Leprechaun	Mystic Green	Arbor Green	Dusty Green
Lima	Lime Yellow	Limeade	True Yellow + Lt Lime
Lisa Pink	Sweetheart Pink	Baby Pink + Spice Pink (T)	Lt Fuchsia
Mellow Yellow	White + Turner's Yellow	Moon Yellow	White + Yellow Oxide (T)
Pale Yellow	Lemonade	Taffy Cream	Lt Yellow
Pine Green	Thicket + Old Ivy 2:1	Evergreen + Midnite Green	Deep Green + Burnt Umber
Poppy Orange	Pure Orange + Red Lt	Cadmium Orange	True Poppy
Rhythm 'n Blue	Night Sky	Blue Violet + Diox Purple	Med Violet + True Lavender
Salem Blue	Cobalt Blue + Buttercream	Salem Blue + Buttermilk 2:1	Med Turquoise + Lt Blue
Salem Green	Aspen Green	Teal Green + Cool Neutral	Dusty Spruce
Straw	Buttercup	Golden Straw	Yellow Ochre + True Yellow
Terra Cotta	Terra Cotta	Terra Cotta + Burnt Orange 3:1	Deep Peach + True Orange
Violet Ice	Lt Periwinkle + White	White + Country Blue	White + True Lavender (T)
White	Titanium White	Snow White	White
Wisteria	Plum Chiffon + White 2:1	Lavender + Cranberry Wine 3:1	Dusty Fuchsia

Paint Conversion Chart

Americana	Delta	Plaid	Aleene
Alizarin Crimson	Black Cherry	Burgundy	Deep Mauve
Antique Gold	Antique Gold	Harvest Gold	Yellow Ochre
Avocado	Dark Jungle	Green Meadow	Deep Sage
Baby Pink	Lisa Pink	Baby Pink	Lt Fuchsia
Berry Red	Cardinal Red	Engine Red	Holiday Red
Bittersweet Chocolate	Dk Burnt Umber	Burnt Umber	Burnt Umber + Black
Boysenberry Pink	Fuchsia	Hot Pink	True Red + White
Brandy Wine	Burgundy Rose	Huckleberry	Dusty Mauve + Deep Mauve
Buttermilk	Antique White	Tapioca	Ivory
Cadmium Orange	Poppy Orange	Red Orange	True Poppy
Country Blue	Blue Lagoon + White	Lt Periwinkle	True Lavender + Dusty Gray + White
Cranberry Wine	Black Cherry + Burgundy Rose (T)	Maroon	Dusty Mauve + Deep Mauve
Deep Midnight Blue	Midnight Blue	Indigo	Deep Blue + Black
Deep Periwinkle	Ultramarine Blue + White	Night Sky + White	Deep Lavender + White
Dioxazine Purple	Purple	Diox Purple	Deep Violet
Evergreen	Forest Green	Thicket	Deep Green + Burnt Umber
Forest Green	Deep River	Shamrock	Deep Green
Golden Straw	Straw	Buttercup	Yellow Oxide + True Yellow
Green Mist	Oasis Green	Poetry Green	Dusty Green
Hauser Dark Green	Hunter Green	Hauser Dark Green	Hunter Green
Hauser Medium Green	Chrome Green Lt + Seminole	Sap Green	Deep Green + Deep Beige
Lamp Black	Black	Licorice	Black
Limeade	Lima	Lime Yellow	Lt Yellow + Lt Lime
Marigold	Empire Gold	Turner's Yellow	Maize
Midnite Green	Black Green	Thicket + Shamrock	Black + Deep Sage
Moon Yellow	Old Parchment	Sunflower	White + True Apricot
Napa Red	Mulberry	Burgundy	Burgundy
Olive Green	Leaf Green + White	Fresh Foliage + Green Olive (T)	Med Yellow + Deep Sage
Orchid	Lilac + Lilac Dust	Orchid	Med Violet + Med Fuchsia
Peach Sherbet	Rosetta	Peach Perfection	True Poppy + White
Peaches 'n Cream	White + Tangerine	Peach Cobbler + Strawberry Parfait	Lt Poppy + True Orange (T)
Plum	Grape	Plum Pudding	Deep Fuchsia + True Gray + White
Pumpkin	Pumpkin	Pure Orange	True Orange
Red Violet	Mendocino + Grape 4:1	Holiday Red + Heather	Deep Fuchsia + True Violet
Royal Fuchsia	Magenta	Fuchsia	True Fuchsia
Santa Red	Tompte Red	Napthol Crimson	True Red
Spice Pink	Pink Parfait	Primrose + Strawberry Parfait	Holiday Red + White
Tangelo Orange	Tangerine	Autumn Leaves	Med Poppy
Tangerine	Yellow + Bittersweet 3:1	Tangerine	True Apricot
Titanium White	White	Titanium White	White
Winter Blue	Wedgwood Blue	Blue Bell + White	White + Dusty Blue

Paint Conversion Chart

Aleene (L)	Delta (D)	Americana (A)	Plaid (P)
Deep Fuchsia	Magenta	Royal Fuchsia	Fuchsia
Deep Sage	Dk Jungle	Avocado	Olive Green
Dusty Green	Alpine	Green Mist	Shamrock + White
Dusty Khaki	Cloudberry + Stonewedge	Sable Brown + Olive Green	Barnwood + Clover
Holiday Red	Fruit Punch	Cadmium Red	Christmas Red
Hunter Green	Hunter Green	Black Forest	Hunter Green
Light Lime	White + Lime Green + Yellow	White + Green + Lemon Yellow	White + Kelly Green + Yellow Lt
Light Yellow	Pale Yellow	Pineapple	Lemon Custard + White
Medium Lavender	Purple + Navy + White	Diox Purple + Navy Blue + White	Night Sky + White
Medium Red	Crimson	Brilliant Red	Red Lt
Medium Turquoise	Cobalt Blue + White	Desert Turquoise + White	Teal + Cobalt + White
Mint	White + Wedgwood Green	Jade Green + White	White + Olive Green
True Apricot	Bittersweet	Tangerine	Tangerine
True Orange	Pumpkin	Pumpkin	Glazed Carrots
True Poppy	Poppy Orange	Cadmium Orange	Terra Cotta + Lt Red Oxide
True Red	Tompte Red	Santa Red	Napthol Crimson

Referred to in projects as Weatherproof, Fade-proof Acrylic Paints

Americana Patio Paints
Blue Bell
Burgundy Rose
Caramel
Carnation
Chive Green
Citrus Green
Cloud White
Fiesta Yellow
Fuchsia
Geranium Red
Golden Honey
Larkspur Blue
Limestone
Olive
Pansy Purple
Patio Brick
Peach Blossom
Pine Green
Red Pepper
Sprout Green
Sunflower Yellow
Sunshine Yellow
Tango Blue
Terra Cotta
Tiger Lily Orange
White
Woodland Brown
Wrought Iron Black

Referred to in projects as Gouache

Jo Sonya Gouache
Aqua
Gold Oxide
Green Oxide
Indian Red Oxide
Iridescent Blue
Iridescent Green
Magenta
Napthol Red Light
Pine Green
Prussian Blue Hue
Raw Sienna
Soft Black
Smoked Pearl
Teal
Titanium White
Turner's Yellow
Ultramarine Blue

Metric Conversion Chart

Inches to Millimetres and Centimetres

Inches	MM	CM	Inches	CM	Inches	CM
⅛	3	0.9	9	22.9	30	76.2
¼	6	0.6	10	25.4	31	78.7
⅜	10	1.0	11	27.9	32	81.3
½	13	1.3	12	30.5	33	83.8
⅝	16	1.6	13	33.0	34	86.4
¾	19	1.9	14	35.6	35	88.9
⅞	22	2.2	15	38.1	36	91.4
1	25	2.5	16	40.6	37	94.0
1¼	32	3.2	17	43.2	38	96.5
1½	38	3.8	18	45.7	39	99.1
1¾	44	4.4	19	48.3	40	101.6
2	51	5.1	20	50.8	41	104.1
2½	64	6.4	21	53.3	42	106.7
3	76	7.6	22	55.9	43	109.2
3½	89	8.9	23	58.4	44	111.8
4	102	10.2	24	61.0	45	114.3
4½	114	11.4	25	63.5	46	116.8
5	127	12.7	26	66.0	47	119.4
6	152	15.2	27	68.6	48	121.9
7	178	17.8	28	71.1	49	124.5
8	203	20.3	29	73.7	50	127.0

Yards to Metres

Yards	Metres	Yards	Metres	Yards	Metres	Yards	Metres	Yards	Metres
⅛	0.11	2⅛	1.94	4⅛	3.77	6⅛	5.60	8⅛	7.43
¼	0.23	2¼	2.06	4¼	3.89	6¼	5.72	8¼	7.54
⅜	0.34	2⅜	2.17	4⅜	4.00	6⅜	5.83	8⅜	7.66
½	0.46	2½	2.29	4½	4.11	6½	5.94	8½	7.77
⅝	0.57	2⅝	2.40	4⅝	4.23	6⅝	6.06	8⅝	7.89
¾	0.69	2¾	2.51	4¾	4.34	6¾	6.17	8¾	8.00
⅞	0.80	2⅞	2.63	4⅞	4.46	6⅞	6.29	8⅞	8.12
1	0.91	3	2.74	5	4.57	7	6.40	9	8.23
1⅛	1.03	3⅛	2.86	5⅛	4.69	7⅛	6.52	9⅛	8.34
1¼	1.14	3¼	2.97	5¼	4.80	7¼	6.63	9¼	8.46
1⅜	1.26	3⅜	3.09	5⅜	4.91	7⅜	6.74	9⅜	8.57
1½	1.37	3½	3.20	5½	5.03	7½	6.86	9½	8.69
1⅝	1.49	3⅝	3.31	5⅝	5.14	7⅝	6.97	9⅝	8.80
1¾	1.60	3¾	3.43	5¾	5.26	7¾	7.09	9¾	8.92
1⅞	1.71	3⅞	3.54	5⅞	5.37	7⅞	7.20	9⅞	9.03
2	1.83	4	3.66	6	5.49	8	7.32	10	9.14

artist
designer
teacher
mother
student

About the Author

I remember the first time I saw a tole-painted item. It was a beautiful tea pot with fruit painted on it. Being somewhat skilled with crafts, I wanted very much to learn this painting technique. After extensive searching, I found a teacher and began a 23-year love affair with my new-found art form.

Since then, I have enjoyed teaching for various shops and conventions. I enjoyed owning my own craft shop—Country Pleasures. With my own designed pattern packets, I have traveled to all the major conventions to display and sell my creations. However, after all these years, I still have not painted a tea pot for myself.

I live in Syracuse, Utah, with husband Reed, who has always been very supportive in all my creative endeavors. We are the proud parents of five sons.

For the past two years, I have been a designer for Chapelle Ltd., doing the work I love.

I would like to thank Jo Packham, Becky Christensen, and the Chapelle staff for making this book a reality.

A special thanks to Amber Hansen for sharing her time, talent, and creativity throughout this book.

I owe a great deal of thanks to Annette Emery for teaching me the basic techniques, necessary strokes, and for giving me a solid foundation on which to create and design on my own.

This book is dedicated to my sweet grandchildren: Ambur, Annie, Alex, Travis, J.D., and Jake. They are always an inspiration and love everything I do.

I hope you enjoy painting the flowers in this book. Remember, always paint with a rainbow in your heart.

Index